NAMES
for Australian
BABIES

NAMES
for Australian
BABIES

PENGUIN BOOKS

Penguin Books Australia Ltd
487 Maroondah Highway, PO Box 257
Ringwood, Victoria 3134, Australia
Penguin Books Ltd
Harmondsworth, Middlesex, England
Penguin Putnam Inc.
375 Hudson Street, New York, New York 10014, USA
Penguin Books Canada Limited
10 Alcorn Avenue, Toronto, Ontario, Canada M4V 3B2
Penguin Books (NZ) Ltd
Cnr Rosedale and Airborne Roads, Albany, Auckland, New Zealand
Penguin Books (South Africa) (Pty) Ltd
5 Watkins Street, Denver Ext 4, 2094, South Africa
Penguin Books India (P) Ltd
11, Community Centre, Panchsheel Park, New Delhi 110 017, India

First published by Penguin Books Australia Ltd 1998

10 9 8 7 6 5 4 3

Design by Scott Williams, Penguin Design Studio
Cover photograph courtesy of the Photo Library of Australia
Typeset in Candida by Midland Typesetters, Maryborough, Victoria
Printed and bound in Australia by Australian Print Group
Maryborough, Victoria

National Library of Australia
Cataloguing-in-Publication data:

Davis, Sarah, 1970– .
   Names for Australian babies.

   New ed.
   ISBN 0 14 027069 8.

   I. Names, Personal – Australia. I. Title.

929.44

CONTENTS

BOYS

A

Aaron From the Hebrew for 'high mountain, lofty', or possibly the Arabic for 'messenger'. Aaron became the first high priest of the Jews and was regarded as a great peacemaker. The variation Aron is often used in Australia, the United States and many European countries; as for instance in Elvis Aron Presley. Other variants include Aarron, Arron, the Hebrew Aharon, Arabic Haroun, Italian Aronne and Aranne and Polish Arek. Pet forms include Ari, Ron and Ronnie.

Abbott From the Hebrew for 'father'. The head of a monastery or abbey is called an abbot. This name was originally used as a surname. Also Abbot, Abott.

Abdi A Muslim name that is popular in Somali, it is a form of Abdul.

Abdul Arabic for 'servant' or 'son'. Also Abdal, Abdoul.

Abdullah Arabic for 'Allah's servant'. Somali variant is Abdalla.

Abe A short form of Abraham.

Abel Probably from the Hebrew for 'the breath' or 'son'. Adam and Eve's second son Abel was killed by his brother Cain.

Abir A Sanskrit Hindu name, it refers to the red powder used in holy festivals.

Abner From the Hebrew for 'Father of light'. The biblical Abner was the commander of King Saul's army. The name was popular after the Reformation as were many other Old Testament biblical names. Variants are Avner and Evner.

Abraham From the Hebrew for 'father of many nations'. Abraham is regarded as the progenitor of the Jewish people. Variants include Abram (which was originally Abraham's name), Ibrahim, Avraham and Avron; shortened forms include Abe, Abie, Ham and Bram.

Ace From the Latin for 'a unit, one'. An 'ace' is the playing card with the highest value; also a term used in tennis, and as an expression of approval, particularly by the young. It is often used as a nickname.

Acton From the Old English for 'oak' and 'village'; a placename meaning 'village with oak trees'.

Adair Probably a Scottish form of Edgar. A surname also used as a personal name.

Adam From the Hebrew for 'red', probably referring to the red earth (*adama*) from which Adam was created. According to the Old Testament book of Genesis, Adam was the first man, created by God after he had made the world. Scottish variants and diminutives of Adam include Adie, Edie and Edom; the Welsh form is Adda; the Spanish Adan, and the Italian form is Adamo.

Adamo Italian form of Adam.

Adan Spanish form of Adam.

Addison From the Anglo-Saxon for 'son of Adam'. A surname that is now also used as a personal name.

Adeeb, Adib Muslim name meaning 'scholarly, literary'.

Aden After a gulf and port in South Yemen or a variant of Aidan.

Adie A pet form of Adam, Adan, Aden and Adrian.

Adolfo Italian name, from the Old German Adolph, meaning 'noble wolf'.

Adonis From the Phoenician *adon* meaning 'lord', a Greek name that is associated with male physical beauty. Adonis was an extremely attractive young man, the god of agriculture, with whom, according to Greek myth, Aphrodite, the goddess of love, was much enamoured.

Adrian From the Latin *Hadrianus*, meaning 'of the Adriatic'. Italian form is Adriano, French form Adrien.

Aeddan A Welsh name for boys. Aeddan was the name of a legendary sixth-century Welsh soldier.

Afan A Welsh name for boys.

Agostino Italian form of Augustine, from the Latin *augustus*, signifying 'celebrated, venerable'.

Ahmed From the Arabic, meaning 'most highly praised'. Also Ahmad.

Aidan An ancient Irish name that comes from *aid*, Gaelic for 'fire'. Aidan was a seventh-century Irish monk. Also Aiden, Aden and Edan.

Aiken From the Old English meaning 'made of oak'.

Ainsleigh, Ainsley, Ainslie Ainslie is Old English for 'a clearing belonging to Annis', now used as a personal name for both boys and girls.

Alain French form of Alan.

Alan, Allan, Allen This is a name of uncertain derivation which may come from the Celtic 'harmony', or the Gaelic 'noble', or 'fair, handsome'. Early versions of the name included the Welsh Alawn and the French Alain. Alan was an early Welsh and Breton saint who became Bishop of Kemper in Brittany.

Alastair Scottish form of Alexander.

Albert From the Old High German name Adelbrecht, meaning 'noble and bright'. The name had quite a complex evolution, but was popularised in English-speaking countries by the German Prince Albert who married Queen Victoria in 1840. It became popular with the British working-class as well as the

Royals. Diminutives are Al, Alby, Bert and Bertie.
European variants include the French Aubert; the
German Albrecht and Bertchen; the Greek Alvertos;
the Italian Alberto and Albertino; the Finnish Alpo;
the Hungarian Bela; and the Latvian Albertas.

Aldo Originally from the Old German for 'old'. A
popular Italian name, and a pet form of names such
as Baldo and Rinaldo.

Alec Short form of Alexander.

Aled A Welsh name, from the name of a river and
lake.

Alex A diminutive of Alexander.

Alexander Greek for 'protector or defender of
humankind'. Like its feminine form Alexandra, the
name has been associated with royalty. Other
famous bearers of the name have included
emperors and popes. Alexander the Great (356–323
BC) was actually the third King Alexanda in
Macedonia, where the name had been adopted by
the royal family, who alternated it with 'Phillip'
each generation. He made huge conquests in Asia,
which led to the wide spread of the name in its
various forms; for instance, many Muslims in India
were named Iksander after him. Diminutives are
Alex, Alexis, Alec, Aleck, Alick and Lex. Scottish
forms include Alastair, now regarded as a name in
its own right, Sanders and Sandy. The French form
is Alexandre, Greek Alexandros and Alekos,
Russian variants include Aleksandr, Lyaksandr,
Sanya, Sasha and Sashenka, Yiddish Aleksander,
Italian Allesandro, German Alexsander, Alik and
Axel, Spanish Alejandro.

Alexis From the Greek 'protector' or 'defender', some
regard it as a variant or diminutive of Alexander.
Used for both sexes. As with Alexander there are

many variants, including the Italian form Alessio;
the Spanish Alejo; the Russian Alexei; the Bulgarian
Aleksi; the French Alexius and Alexe; the
Hungarian Elek; and the Latvian Aleksis.

Alfio An Italian name derived from the Latin *alfius*,
meaning white.

Alfonso A popular Italian boys' name, it is a variant
of the Spanish Alphonso (from the Old German for
'noble and ready').

Alfred From the Old English, from *aelf*, meaning 'elf'
and *raed* meaning 'council', elf council, implying
'wise as a supernatural being'. The elves were
white spirits, beautiful wise imaginary beings who
could influence the lives of human beings. Alfred
the Great (849–901), who repelled the invading
Danes from southern England, was a great leader
and scholar. Diminutives are Alf and Alfie. An
Italian form is Alfrédo and a popular Norwegian
variant is Alf.

Alistair, Alister Gaelic variations of Alexander (from
the Greek for 'protector or defender of men').

Alejandro A Spanish form of Alexander, also found in
America.

Allard Old English for 'highborn and brave'. Also
Alard, Ellard and pet form Al.

Alwyn Welsh name from the Old English Aethelwine,
meaning 'noble friend.' Also spelt Alvin and Alwin.

Amir Somali name meaning 'born in abundant times'.

Anand Hindu name meaning 'joyful'.

Anastasios From the Greek for 'resurrection'. See
Anastasia.

Anatoli, Anatoly Russian form of Anatole, Anatolius.

Anatole, Anatolius From the Greek meaning 'from the
east'.

Anders Scandinavian form of Andrew.

André French form of Andrew.

Andres Spanish form of Andrew.

Andreas Greek form of Andrew.

Andrew From the Greek *andreios* meaning 'manly'.
Pet forms include Andy, Andie and Drew. Among
its Russian variants are Andrei, Andrej, Andrey,
Andreyka, Andrik, Andriyechko and Andresej.
Other variants include the French and Portuguese
André; the German and Greek Andreas; the Polish
Andrezej and Aniol; the Swedish and Norwegian
Anders; the Czech Ondrej and Ondro; the Croatian
Andrija; the Serbian Andreja; the Spanish Andres;
and the Ukrainian Andriy and Andruno.

Angel From the Greek *angelos* for messenger or
angel. The name has been popular for men in
Spanish-speaking countries for centuries, and is also
found in the United States.

Angelico, Angelo, Agnolo Italian forms of Angelo.

Angelo Greek 'angel' or 'messenger', which came to
mean a bringer of good news to man from God. It is
probable that 'Angelos' was initially given as a
surname in the Byzantine Empire.

Angus A popular Scottish name, it came from the
Gaelic 'Aonghus' for 'unique or only choice'. In the
third century BC Aonghus was said to be one of the
three Irish brothers who invaded and ruled
Scotland, bequeathing his name to the cattle
Aberdeen Angus.

Anian Welsh name meaning 'personality,
temperament'.

Anthony, Antony From the Roman clan name Antonius,
it came to mean 'priceless'. Antonius Marcus, known
as Mark Antony, was a popular Roman statesman in
the first century BC. The spelling with 'h' appeared in
the sixteenth century. The diminutive is Tony.

Variants include the Italian Antonio and Anton; the Czech Antonin and Tonda; the French Antoine; and the Polish Antoni, Antek and Antos.

Antoine French form of Anthony.

Antoni Polish form of Anthony.

Apollo From the Greek for 'destroyer'. In classical mythology Apollo, son of Zeus, was the symbol of light, the god of song and music, and through the Delphic Oracle, prophecy and healing.

Arawn Welsh name for boys. Arawn was King of the Underworld in the tales of the Mabinogi.

Archibald From the Teutonic Eorconbald, meaning 'truly bold'. Archibald is most prevalent in Scotland where the name is very popular with the Douglas and Campbell clans. Diminutive is Archie.

Aren A Nigerian name meaning 'eagle'.

Arial Welsh name for boys meaning 'strength' or 'valour'.

Arjun Hindu boys' name meaning 'bright'. Arjun was one of the Pandava princes of the *Mahabharata*.

Arkady, Arki, Arkie A Russian name for boys.

Armaan Muslim name meaning 'wish, hope'.

Armand French variant of Herman, from the Old German for 'army man' or 'soldier'.

Armando Spanish form of Armand.

Arnold From the Old German *arnwalt*, meaning 'eagle power'. The Normans brought it to Britain in the form of Arnaud or Aunaut, and it gradually evolved to Arnold. The Welsh variant is Arnallt; the French Arnaud and Aunaut; the Italian and Spanish Arnoldo.

Art A popular diminutive of Arthur.

Arthur Of uncertain origins. The theories include that it may have come from the Celtic 'the strength of a bear', the Irish *art* for 'rock', the Norse 'follower of

Thor' the war god, or it may be a form of a Roman name, such as the clan name Artorius. The legendary King Arthur united Britain in the ninth century. Art, Artie and Arty are diminutives.

Artro   Welsh name for boys.

Arturo   An Italian form of Arthur.

Asad   Muslim name meaning 'lion'.

Asher   Hebrew name meaning 'happy one'.

Ashlee, Ashley, Ashleigh, Ashlie   From the Old English, from *aesc*, ash tree. The name means 'from the meadow of ash trees', and was originally given as a surname to a person who lived there. Also used as a girls' name.

Ashton   Old English placename meaning 'ash tree settlement'.

Astin   See Austen.

Athol   Originally from the Scottish placename Atholl, this became a surname and, in the nineteenth century, a personal name.

Attilio   Italian form of Attila, a Gothic name meaning 'little father'.

Auberon   See Oberon.

Aubert   French form of Albert.

Augustine   From the Latin *augustus*, meaning 'venerable'.

Austen, Austin, Austyn   A variant of Augustine.

Avery   A form of Alfred.

Avi   From the Hebrew for 'divine father', an Israeli name.

Axel   From the Old German, meaning 'father of peace'.

Azriel   Israeli name from the Hebrew for 'God is my salvation'.

B

Babur A Muslim name meaning 'lion'.

Baden From the German for 'bather'.

Bailey From the Old French for 'bailiff'. Also spelt Bayley.

Baldwin From the Old German for 'courageous friend'. Maldwyn is the Welsh form.

Barclay Old English 'from the birch tree meadow'. Also Berkeley.

Barnaby Aramaic for son of exhortation. The original form, Barnabas, was the name of an apostle. The short form is Barney, often used in its own right.

Barnard, Barnet, Barnett See Bernard.

Barrett, Barett, Barret From the Old German for 'bear rule'.

Barry Irish for 'spear'. In modern usage, also a popular diminutive of such names as Bernard, Barnaby. Also spelt Barrie. Popular diminutives include Baz and Bazza.

Bart See Bartholomew.

Bartholomew A Hebrew name meaning 'son of Talmai'—son of the furrow. St Bartholomew is supposed to have been Nathanael. Known as Bartolomé in Spanish; Barthélemy in French; Bartholdy in German; Bartholomej in Czech.

Barton A diminutive of Bartholomew.

Baseer Muslim name meaning 'intelligent'.

Basil 'Kingly', from the Greek *basileios*, but owes its use to three Eastern saints. Also a herb. Illyrian and Russian forms include Vasilis, Vasilij and Vasily; the Spanish is Basilio.

Basilio Spanish form of Basil.

Baxter Old English for 'baker'.

Baz   Diminutive of Barry.

Beagan   Irish for 'small one'.

Beattie   From the Latin, 'bringer of gladness'. Also
Beatty and Beaty.

Beau   French for 'handsome' and a popular
diminutive of Beauregard. Sometimes spelt Bo.

Beauregard   From the Old French meaning 'beautiful
expression'.

Ben   Diminutive of Benedict or Benjamin.

Benedict   From the Latin, meaning 'blessed'.
Benedikt is an old variant form of the name. Its
English variants include Ben, Bennet, Bennett,
Benny, Dick. The French form is Benôit, Benoist;
the Italian Benedik, Benci, Benke; the Portuguese
Bento; the Russian Venedikt, Venka, Venya,
Benedo; and the Spanish forms include Benedicto,
Beni, Benito and Benitin.

Beniamino   Italian form of Benjamin.

Benito   Spanish form of Benedict.

Benjamin   A name from the Old Testament meaning
'son of the right hand', thus representing strength
and fortune. The Arabic form is Binyamin. Short
forms are Ben, Benjie or Benny.

Benjie, Benjy   Diminutives of Benjamin.

Beppi, Beppo   Italian and Spanish pet names for
Joseph.

Bergen   Scandinavian, meaning 'lives on the hill'.
Bergen is also a major port in Norway. The variants
include Bergin and Birgin.

Berkeley   Old English meaning 'birch wood'. Also
spelt Barclay.

Bernard   Old German meaning 'strong or brave as a
bear'. Beornheard in Anglo-Saxon means 'bear-
hard'. The Italian form is Bernardo; the Irish
Berneen; the German Bernhard; and its Dutch form

is Bernhart. Popular diminutives include Barney and Bernie.

Bernardo Italian form of Bernard.

Bert See Albert, Bertram, Bertrand, Gilbert, Herbert, Robert.

Bertram, Bertrand Bertram is Old German for 'bright raven' and Bertrand 'bright shield', but commonly regarded as variants of the same name. Its diminutives include Bart, Bert or Bertie. Bertuccio is the Italian form of Bertram.

Bevan Welsh for 'Son of Evan'.

Bill, Billy Pet forms of William.

Binh Vietnamese for 'peace'.

Birch Old English for 'grove of birch trees'.

Björn A Scandinavian form of Bernard, 'brave as a bear'.

Blade Anglo-Saxon 'fame, good fortune'.

Blain(e), Blane, Blayne Irish for 'thin and lean'.

Blair Both a Scottish placename and a surname, meaning 'marshy plain'. Irish for 'child of the fields', and often given to those born under the earth signs.

Blaise, Blaize, Blase, Blaze Two possible origins: from the Greek *basileios*, 'royal', or the Latin *blaeseus* 'stuttering, deformed'. Also the name of Arthurian knight Merlin's secretary, and the French philosopher, Pascal. Also Blaisot in the French; Blasius in German; Ballas in Hungarian; and Blazej in Polish.

Blake A surname meaning 'dark-complexioned, black', Blake is also used as a first name.

Blue Either from the colour or a nickname.

Bo A variant spelling of Beau.

Bob, Bobbie, Bobby Diminutives of Robert.

Bohdan Ukranian form of Donald, meaning 'world

13

ruler'. Also Bogdan, Bogdashka, Danya.

Bond   Old English meaning 'tiller of the soil'.

Borg   Scandinavian name meaning 'one who lives in a castle'.

Boris   A Russian name meaning 'fight', from an old Slav word *borotj*.

Botan   Japanese for 'peony'.

Bowen   Irish for 'small, victorious one', or Old Welsh for 'the well-born or youthful one's son'. Diminutives include Bow, Bowie.

Boyce   Old French, meaning 'son of the forest'.

Boyd   Scottish Gaelic name, meaning 'yellow-haired'.

Brad   Diminutive of Bradford, Braden, Bradley or Brady, also a name in its own right.

Braden   Old English for 'from the wide valley'.

Bradford   Old English for 'from the wide river crossing'.

Bradley   Derives from the Old English surname meaning 'broad clearing'. Brad, Brady and Lee are short forms.

Brady   Diminutive of Bradley.

Brae   Scottish for 'hill'.

Bram   Diminutive of Abraham.

Brand   From the Old English, meaning 'firebrand'. Also a diminutive of Brandon. Related forms are Brandt and Brant.

Brandeis   From the Czechoslovakian, meaning 'dweller on a burnt clearing' or 'one who comes from Brandeis'. Variants include Brand, Brandt, Brandy and Brant.

Brandon, Brandan   From the Old English, meaning 'one from the beacon hill'. Diminutives and variants include Bran, Brand, Brannon and Brandum. See also Brendan.

Brannon   A variant of Brandon.

Brencis Latvian form of Lawrence, meaning 'crowned with laurel'.

Brendan, Brendon In Irish Brendan means 'little raven' or 'brave and bold'. In German it means 'aflame'. Brandon is often a variant. Also spelt Brandan or Brendon.

Brent, Brentan, Brenton, Brentyn Originally a surname meaning 'burnt' in the Old English or 'hill, high place', from a West Country placename.

Bret, Brett From the surname Briton or Breton; Brett is literally Celtic for 'from Britannia'.

Brian, Brien, Bryan A Celtic name of uncertain meaning, though it has been variously linked to *bre*, 'hill' and with *brigh*, 'strength'. Bryan is a variant spelling of the name.

Brice, Bryce Celtic for 'son of Rhys'. St Brice was a Bishop of Tours.

Brock Old English for 'badger'.

Broderick Scottish and Norse for 'brother'. Diminutives include Brodi, Brodie and Brody. See also Roderick.

Brodie, Brody Scottish for 'ditch'. Brodie is the name of a Scottish castle. Also the short form of Broderick.

Bron Afrikaans for 'source'.

Bronislav, Bronislaw Slavic for 'glorious weapon'.

Bronson English and German for 'brown son'. Diminutive is Bron.

Brooks English for 'running water' or 'stream'.

Bruce Old French for 'brushwood grove'. Bruis or Braose (now Brieuse) is a village with a castle near Cherbourg.

Bruno German for 'brown-skinned'.

Bryan A form of Brian.

Bryce A variant of Brice.

Bryn From the same root as Brian, from the Welsh for 'hill'. Brynmor means 'big hill'.

Buck, Buckley Old English for 'male deer'.

Bud, Buddy Slang for 'buddy' or 'brother', now a name in its own right.

Burgess Old English from the Teutonic, meaning 'citizen of a fortified town'.

Burke, Berke, Bourke Old English for 'fort, manor'.

Burleigh, Burley Old English for 'clearing with a fort or manor'. Burl is a diminutive.

Burnum Aboriginal for 'great warrior'. Burnum Burnum is the name of an Aboriginal activist.

Burt 'Shining and glorious' in Old English. See also Albert, Bertram, Gilbert, Herbert, Robert.

Burton English 'hill' or 'borough town'. Also Bert, Berton, Burt.

Byron Meaning 'at the cattle sheds', from the same root as the English 'byre'.

C

Cadel, Cadfael The Welsh *cad* means 'battle'. Cadfael means 'battle metal' (also the hero of Ellis Peter's medieval mysteries).

Caesar Latin for 'hairy' or 'long-haired one', which over time has taken on the meaning 'emperor'. English variants are Cesar and Cesare; the Bulgarian are Casar, Cezar, Kaiser; Cezary and Cezek are the Polish; Cesareo, Cesareo and Sariot the Spanish.

Cai Welsh form of Caius.

Cain From the Hebrew for 'spear'. The name of

Adam and Eve's elder son, who killed his brother
Abel.

Caio   Welsh form of Caius.

Caiseal   An Irish name, from the city of Cashel, the
ancient capital of Munster province.

Caius   A Roman first name that comes from the Latin
gaudere, 'to rejoice'. Still in use in Wales in the
forms Cai, Caio and Caw.

Caleb   From the Hebrew for 'bold and impetuous' or
'a dog'. In the Bible the son of Jephunneh.
Diminutives and variations include Cal, Cale and
Kaleb. The Arabic is Kalb.

Callum, Calum   See Malcolm.

Calvin   From the French meaning 'bald'. A name first
used in honour of Jean Cauvin, famous for his strict
morality.

Cam   English gypsy for 'beloved'. Short form of
Cameron.

Cameron   A Scottish clan name, from the Gaelic for
'crooked nose'.

Campbell   A Scottish name, with the meaning
'crooked mouth'. Campbell is a very famous Scottish
clan.

Carey   Latin meaning is 'dear, costly' or Old Welsh
for 'one who lives at the castle'. Cary is an
alternative spelling.

Carl   Short form of Charles.

Carlos   Spanish form of Charles.

Carroll   Irish form of Charles, meaning 'champion
warrior'.

Carson   From the Old English, meaning 'son of the
marsh-dwellers'.

Carter   Old English for 'a cart driver'. Originally a
surname, now used as a first name.

Cary   Popular form of Carey.

Casey   An Irish surname, 'descendant of the vigilant one' or 'brave'. Popular short form of Casimir.

Casimir   Old Slavic for 'he announces or commands peace'. Kazimir in the Bulgarian, Czech, German and Russian; Kazmer in Hungarian; Kazek, Kazik and Kazio in the Polish.

Casper   Persian for 'master of the treasure'. See also Jasper.

Cass   Modern form of Casper.

Cassidy   From the Irish, meaning 'ingenious, clever'. Also Cassady.

Cassius   From the Latin, meaning 'vain'. Cassius Clay is the real name of the boxer Muhammad Ali.

Cecil   From the Latin Sextilius, which was rendered Seisyllt in Old Welsh. This in turn became the family name Cecil, and is now more usually a first name.

Cedric   Perhaps a misreading of Cerdic, an early Saxon name meaning 'amiable'. There is a Welsh name Cedrych, meaning 'pattern of bounty'.

Cedrych   Welsh form of Cedric.

Chad   A sixth-century Anglo-Saxon saint. From the Old English *cadda*, 'warlike one' or 'related to Mars'.

Chaim   Hebrew for 'life'. The Hebrew form is Hyam, Polish Chaimek and Haim, and the Russian is Khaim.

Chandler   Old French for 'candlemaker'.

Charles   *Carl* was the Old German word and Anglo-Saxon *Ceorl* for 'a man', later latinised as Carolus, and Charles in French. Variants include Carl or Karl (German and Scandinavian); the eastern European form is Carol or Karel. Short forms include Charl, Charley, Charlie (the pet Scottish form), Chuck and Chas.

Charlie, Charley   Variant of Charles.

Charlton A variant of Carlton, a place and surname meaning 'settlement of the free men or peasants'. Carleton is an alternative spelling.

Chay Scottish variant of Charles.

Chen Chinese for 'vast' or 'great'.

Chester From the Latin *castra*, meaning 'a camp'. The Old English meaning is 'living at a fortified army camp'. Variants and diminutives are Ches, Cheston and Chet.

Chet Diminutive of Chester.

Chetwin Derived from an Old English placename, meaning 'little house on the twisted path'.

Chowdhury A Muslim name meaning 'landowner'.

Chris A diminutive of Christopher and Christian.

Christian Greek for 'believer in Christ, the anointed one'. Variants include Christos, Christiaan, Christiano and Kerstan.

Christie, Christy Diminutives of Christopher.

Christopher Christopher means 'Christ carrier', the patron saint of wayfarers. Chris or Kit are popular diminutives.

Cinead See Kenneth.

Clancy From the Irish, meaning 'ruddy warrior'.

Clarence From the Latin for 'famous'. An alternate source is the fourteenth-century dukedom. A related name is Sinclair.

Clark, Clarke An occupational surname, meaning 'cleric, scholar'.

Claud A variant of Claude.

Claude From the original Latin Claudius, a clan name meaning 'limping'. The feminine forms are Claudette, Claudia and Claudine. Alternate forms include Claudan, Claudell, Claudien, Claudio, Claudius and Klaudio.

Claudius See Claude.

Claus A diminutive of Nicholas. A related form is Klaus. See Nicholas.

Clayton From an Old English surname and placename, *claeg*, meaning 'clay' and *tun*, 'settlement'.

Clement Derived from the Latin *clemens*, 'merciful'. One of St Paul's fellow-labourers. Short forms are Clem and Clim. The German form is Klemens and Menz; the Italian Clemente and Clemenza; the Polish Klemens and Klimek; the Russian Klim, Kliment and Klimka; and the Spanish Clemen, Clemente and Clemento. Feminine forms are Clementina and Clementine.

Cliff A short form of Clifford or Clifton.

Clifford An aristocratic name originally given to someone living near a cliff or ford. Cliff is a common diminutive.

Clifton From a surname and a place, from the Old English meaning 'settlement on a cliff'.

Clint Short form of Clinton, made popular by the actor Clint Eastwood.

Clinton An aristocratic surname used as a first name. The name is probably a corruption of Glympton, a settlement on the river Glyme, or from the Old English, meaning 'settlement on a hill'.

Clive First recorded as a placename in Shropshire in 1327. Its meaning is a variation of 'cliff dweller'.

Clyde After the Scottish river. A surname now used as a first name.

Cole A diminutive of Nicholas.

Colin, Collin In medieval France Colin was a diminutive of Nicholas. Its Celtic meaning, 'a young hound', is derived from *cailean*.

Collwyn The Welsh form of Colin.

Colm See Malcolm.

Conan Gaelic name meaning 'hound or wolf' or 'high'. Possibly a Breton name that passed into Irish use.

Connall A popular ancient Celtic name meaning 'the strength of a wolf'. The name of many celebrated Irish warriors.

Connor The anglicised form of the Gaelic *Conchobar*, meaning 'high desire'; the name of the king of Ulster in the *Tain*. Also Conor.

Conrad The anglicised form of the German Konrad, meaning 'bold counsel'. Diminutives include Curt and Kurt.

Conroy From the Irish Gaelic, meaning 'wise man'.

Constantine From the Latin *constans*, meaning 'constant'. The name borne by several Roman and Byzantine emperors.

Conway From the Welsh, meaning 'holy river'.

Cooper From an Old English occupational surname, 'barrel maker'. Coop is a short form.

Corbet, Corbett Derived from the Latin for 'dark as a raven'. Variants include Corbie, Corbin and Cory.

Cordell An occupational name, meaning 'rope maker'.

Corey An Irish Gaelic placename, meaning 'the hollow'. Also a surname. Variants are Correy, Corrie and Corrye.

Cormac Obscure origins, but possibly Gaelic for 'charioteer' and 'son of the raven'. Related forms are Cormick and Cormack.

Cornel Short form of Cornelius, meaning 'like a horn'.

Cornelius From the Roman clan name, probably derived from the Latin *cornu*, meaning 'war horn'. The feminine form is Cornelia.

Cory See Corey.

Cosmo   After St Cosmas, the patron saint of physicians, whose name is derived from *kosmos*, 'order'. The Italian form is Cosimo.

Coulson   A surname derived from Nicholas.

Courtney, Courtenay   An aristocratic surname used as a first name. The name is thought of and used as a nickname, *court nez* meaning 'short nose'.

Craig   From the Gaelic, meaning 'cliff', and still used in Scotland in that sense.

Crawford   From the Old English placename, meaning 'ford of the crows'. Used as both a surname and a given name.

Creighton   From an Old English placename, meaning 'rocky spot'. Also Crichton.

Cresswell   After an Old English placename, 'well where the watercress grows'.

Crichton   See Creighton.

Crosby   A Scandinavian placename, meaning 'at the cross'. Also spelt Crosbie.

Crowther   From an Old English occupational surname meaning 'fiddler'.

Curt   A diminutive of Curtis, an alternative spelling of Kurt and a form of Conrad.

Curtis   A name derived from the French *curteis*, 'courteous'.

Cuthbert   After a seventh-century bishop of Lindisfarne, meaning 'well-known, famous'.

Cyril   A name of Greek derivation, connected to the word *kyrios*, meaning 'lord'. Welsh form is Girioel, and the only short form is Cy.

Cyrus   Probably from the Persian word for 'throne'.

D

Dacey From the Irish Gaelic, meaning 'from the south'. In Latin meaning 'from Dacia', an area that is now Romania. Variants include Dacian, Dacy, Daicey, Daicy.

Dafydd The Welsh form of David.

Daimen See Damon.

Dale From the Old English placename, meaning 'valley'. Originally a surname meaning 'one who lives in the valley'. Variants include Daley and Dayle.

Daly From the Irish Gaelic, meaning 'assembly'. Variants include Daley and Dawley.

Dallas From the Scottish Gaelic, a placename of a village in north-eastern Scotland, used as a first name since the nineteenth century.

Dalton From the Old English placename meaning 'the settlement in the valley'. Variants include Dallton and Dalten.

Damian From the Greek name Damianos, possibly 'to tame', although the Greek root is also close to the word for 'spirit'. Variants include Daemon, Daimen, Daimon, Daman, Damen, Dameon, Damiano, Damien, Damion, Damon, Damyan, Damyen and Damyon.

Damon The French form of Damian.

Dan A diminutive of Daniel.

Daniel From the Hebrew, meaning 'God is my judge'. In the famous Old Testament story, Daniel is thrown into a den of lions because he insists on praying to his God while a captive in Babylon; he was of course rescued by the same God. Other variants include Dan, Danal, Dane, Daneal, Dani,

Danial, Daniele, Dannel, Dannie, Danny, Danyal and Danyel. The feminine forms are Dana, Danette, Daniella, Danielle and Danita.

Danny A diminutive of Daniel, often used as a name in its own right.

Dante From the Latin Durante, the Italian form of Durand, meaning 'lasting, enduring'. The name is borne by the Italian poet Dante Alighieri (1265–1321).

Darby From the Old English placename, meaning 'park with deer'. Derived from Derby, a surname used as a first name. Darby is occasionally used for girls. Variants include Darbie and Derby.

Darcy From a surname introduced in Britain at the time of the Norman Conquest, from the French placename Arcy. Also Irish Gaelic for 'dark'.

Darius From the Greek, meaning 'rich'. Darius the great was an emperor of Persia in the fifth century BC.

Darnell From the Old English placename, meaning 'the hidden spot'. Another variant is Darnall.

Darrel Possibly originated as a French placename, like Darcy. Variants include Darral, Darrell, Darrill, Darrol, Darryl, Daryl, Derril, Deryl and Deryll.

Darren From the Irish Gaelic, meaning 'great'. Variants include Darrin, Darran, Daron, Daren, Darin, Darron, Darryn and Derron.

Daryl see Darrel.

Dave A diminutive of David.

David From the Hebrew, meaning 'dear one'. In the Old Testament, the young David used his slingshot to kill the mighty giant Goliath, and went on to become King of Israel and author of the Psalms. He has been a favourite subject of artists, notably sculptors of the Italian Renaissance, like

Michelangelo and Donatello. St David is the patron
saint of Wales, and in Scotland, David was a royal
name. Variants include Dafydd, Dai, Dave, Davey,
Davidde, Davide, Davidson, Davie, Davin, Davis,
Daven, Davon and Davy.

Davis   From the Old English, meaning 'David's son'.
Contraction of surname that cropped up in the
Middle Ages. Variants include Dave, Davidson,
Davies, Davison and Davy.

Dawson   From the Old English, meaning 'David's
son'. Another form of the medieval surname.

Dean   From the Old English placename, meaning
'valley'. Variants include Deane, Deen, Dene, Deyn
and Dino.

Declan   Meaning is uncertain, but possibly after the
name of a sixth-century Irish saint.

Delmore   From the Old French, meaning 'of the sea'.
Other variants include Delmar, Delmer and Delmor.

Delroy   From the French, meaning 'the king'. Other
forms are Elroy and Leroy. Another variant is
Delroi.

Delwin   From the Old English, meaning 'proud friend'
or 'bright friend'. Variants include Dalwin, Delavan,
Delevan, Dellwin, Delwyn and Delwynn.

Dempsey   From the Irish Gaelic, meaning 'proud'. A
variant is Dempsy.

Dempster   From the Old English, meaning 'one who
judges'.

Denham   From the Old English placename, meaning
'village in a valley'.

Denholm   From the Scottish placename and surname,
ultimately from the Old English *denu*, meaning
'valley' and *holm*, 'island'.

Dennis   From the Greek, meaning 'follower of
Dionysius'. Dionysius was the classical Greek god of

wine, but the name also appears in the New
Testament. St Denis is the patron saint of France.
Some variants include Den, Denies, Denis, Dennes,
Dennet, Denney, Dennie, Dennison, Denny, Dennys,
Denys, Deon, Dion, Dionisio, Dionysius and Dionysus.

Denny   From the diminutive Dennis.

Denton   From the Old English placename, meaning
'settlement in the valley'.

Denver   From the Old English placename, meaning
'green valley'.

Derby   See Darby.

Derek, Derrick, Deryck, Deryk   From the Old German,
meaning 'the people's ruler'. All variants of
Theodoric.

Dermot   From the Irish name Diarmuid or Diarmait,
meaning 'free from envy'. Also Dermott, Diarmid
and Diarmuid.

Derreck   See Derek.

Derry   A diminutive of Derek, sometimes associated
with an Irish placename.

Deryn   A Welsh name of obscure origin, probably
from *aderyn*, meaning 'bird'.

Des   A diminutive of Desmond.

Desmond   From the Irish Gaelic Deas Mumhaim,
meaning 'from South Munster', an ancient kingdom
in Ireland. Also Desmund.

Devlin   From the Irish Gaelic, meaning 'brave', 'of
fierce valour'. Variants are Devland, Devlen and
Devlyn.

Dewi   A Welsh form of David. Also spelt Dewey.

Dexter   From the Latin *dexter*, meaning 'right-
handed', or the Old English for 'dyer'.

Dick, Dicky, Dickie   Diminutives of Richard.

Dickson   A variant of Richard and a variant spelling
of Dixon.

Diego   The Spanish form of Jacob.

Digby   From the Old Norse, meaning 'town by the ditch'.

Dillon   From the Irish Gaelic, meaning 'faithful'. Sometimes used as a variant spelling of Dylan.

Dimitri   From the Greek, meaning 'belonging to Demeter', the goddess of fertility. Other forms of the name include Demeter, Demetrius, Dimitry, Demetre, Dimitrios, Dimos, Takis and Dmitri.

Dion   A variant of Dennis. The feminine forms are Dione and Dionne.

Dirk   A variant of Derek.

Dixon   From the Old English, meaning 'son of Dick'. Also rendered Dickson.

Dominic, Dominick   From the Latin *dominicus*, 'of the Lord' or 'born on Sunday'. St Dominic is the founder of a monastic order. English short forms and variants are Dom, Domenic, Nick, Nicky; the French is Dominique; the Czechoslovakian Dominik, Dumin; the Italian Domenico, Domingo and Menico; the Polish Niki; the Portuguese Domingos; the Spanish Domicio, Domingo and Mingo. The feminine forms are Dominica and Dominique.

Don   Short form of Donald and Donovan.

Donald   From the Irish Gaelic name Domhnall, meaning 'world' and 'mighty'. Its short forms are Don, Donnie and Donny.

Donato   From the Latin for 'a gift'. The Italian form is Donatello.

Donovan   Derived from an Irish surname, meaning 'dark warrior'. The diminutives are Don and Donny.

Dorian   From the Greek *dorios*, meaning 'child of the sea' or 'of Doros', a legendary Greek hero.

Doug   Short form of Douglas.

Douglas   Derived from a Scottish surname and a

placename, ultimately from the Gaelic *dubhglas*,
meaning 'dark water'. Diminutives are Doug, Dugie
and Dougie.

Drew   A diminutive of Andrew.

Duane   From an Irish surname, meaning 'black'. Also
spelt Dwayne.

Dudley   From the Old English, meaning 'one from the
people's meadow'.

Duncan   From an Irish name meaning 'brown
warrior'. The name was borne by two Scottish kings
of the eleventh century.

Dustin   From the Old German, meaning 'a fighter'.
The diminutive is Dusty.

Dwayne   See Duane.

Dwight   From a surname of uncertain origin, possibly
a diminutive of Dionysius (see Dennis).

Dylan   A Welsh name, meaning 'son of the wave'.
Dylan Thomas was a poet.

E

Eamon, Eamonn   Irish form of Edmund. Also spelt
Eammon.

Earl   From the Old English for 'nobleman'. Variations
include Earle and Errol.

Earnest   A form of Ernest, from the Old German
meaning 'vigour' or 'earnestness'. Variations include
Ernst, Ernesto, Ernis and Ernest. The French form is
Erneste; the Spanish and Italian Ernesto. Ern and
Ernie are short forms.

Ebenezer   From the Hebrew, meaning 'stone of help'.

Edan   Celtic for 'fire', sometimes used for a boy born

under the fire signs. Also a form of Aidan.

Eddy Scandinavian for 'unresting'. Also a short form of Edgar or Edward.

Eden Hebrew name meaning 'delight'.

Edgar Old English for 'rich, happy' and 'spear'. Short forms are Ed, Eddie, Ned and Neddy. The French form is Edgard; the Italian is Edgardo; the Lithuanian Edgaras.

Edmond The French form of Edmund.

Edmund Old English name meaning 'wealthy, happy'. Short forms are the same as for Edgar. The Irish form is Eamon; the Italian Edmondo; the Spanish Edmundo; and the Hungarian Odi or Odon.

Edward Old English for 'wealthy guardian'. Eduard is used in Czechoslovakia, Germany, Poland, Canada and the US; the Portuguese form is Eduardo or Duarte; the Swedish, Norwegian and Danish form is Edvard; and the French form is Edouard.

Edwin Old English for 'happy, rich' and 'friend'. Variants include Eduino and Edvinas; short forms are Ed, Eddie and Win.

Eirik The Norse form of Eric.

Eldred Old English for 'old' and 'counsel'. Variants include Aldred and Eldridge.

Elgar Old English for 'noble elf'.

Eli Hebrew for 'Jehovah' and 'the highest one'. Also a diminutive of Elijah and Elisha.

Elijah Hebrew for 'Jehovah is God'. Other variants are Elias, Elija, Elijas, Elio, Eliott, Ellis, Ilja, Ilya and Ilyas.

Eliot A modern form of Elias and Elijah. Also spelt Elliott.

Ellis Modern form of Elias.

Elmer From the Old English name Aylmer, meaning 'noble' and 'famous'. Also spelt Elmar.

Elmo Italian and Greek name meaning 'amiable'.

Elmore English name meaning 'a moor where the elm trees grow'.

Elroy Spanish for 'the king'. Sometimes used as an alternate form of Delroy and Leroy.

Elton Old English 'from the old town'.

Elvin A form of Alvin, meaning 'elf' and 'noble' and 'friend'.

Elvis From the Old English, a form of Elvin.

Elwin, Elwyn Welsh meaning for 'white browed'.

Emerson Son of Emery.

Emery Teutonic for 'hardworking ruler'. Other English variants are Emerson, Emmery and Emory; the Czechoslovakian is Imrich; and the Hungarian is Imre.

Émil Gothic for 'industrious' or Latin for 'flatterer'. Czechoslovakian forms are Milo and Emilek; the French is Émile; the Italian, Portuguese and Spanish form is Emilio; and the Welsh is Emlyn.

Emlyn Welsh form of Émil.

Emmanuel Hebrew, meaning 'God is with us'. Variants of the name are Emmanouil, Immanuele, Molis, Manuel, Manuelo and Manoly.

Emmett German for 'industrious', 'strong'.

Endre Hungarian form of Andrew.

Engelbert Old German for 'bright angel'. Short forms include Bert, Bertie, Berty, Ingelbert and Inglebert.

Enoch Hebrew name meaning 'educated' or 'dedicated'.

Enright Irish for 'son of the attacker'.

Enriqué Spanish and Portuguese form of Henry.

Eric, Erik Old Norse name meaning 'ever powerful' or 'eternal ruler'. Variants include Eirik, Erich (German and Czechoslovakian), Eriks (Latvian and

Russian) and Erico (Italian). Rick and Ricky are
short forms.

Ernest   See Earnest.

Ernie   Short form of Earnest and Ernest.

Errol   A German form of Earl.

Erskine   Gaelic name meaning 'projecting height'.

Esteban   Spanish form of Stephen.

Ethan   Hebrew meaning 'firm and strong'.

Étienne   French form of Stephen.

Euan   A form of Ewen.

Eugene   Greek for 'well-born' or 'noble', sometimes
Eugène. Gene is a short form and also a name in
its own right. Other forms include Zenda
(Czechoslovakian); Zhenka, Zheka, Evgeny and
Yevgeniy (Russian); and Egen (Swedish).

Evan   Welsh form of John, meaning 'young warrior'
or 'young bowman'. Short forms or variations
include Ewan and Owen.

Evelyn   A surname sometimes used as a masculine
name (for instance, Evelyn Waugh), but more
usually as a girls' name.

Everard   Old German name meaning 'boar' and
'hardy'.

Everett   A variation of Everard.

Ewan   The Scottish form of Eugene. Other forms
include Euan and Ewen.

Ewart   An English contraction of Everard.

Ewen   Celtic for 'well-born youth', also a form of
Ewan.

Euan   A form of Ewen.

Ezra   Hebrew for 'helper', 'strong'.

F

Fabian Latin family name meaning 'bean grower'. The French forms are Fabien and Fabert; the Italian Fabio and Fabiano; the Latvian Fabius and the German Faber.

Fabrizio Italian name meaning 'craftsman'.

Fairleigh Old English, meaning 'from the bull meadow' or 'from the ram meadow'. Variations are Fairlay, Fairlie, Farley, Lee and Leigh.

Faisal Arabic for 'decisive'. Also Faisel, Faizal and Fayzel.

Falkner English, meaning 'trainer of falcons'. Variations include Falconer, Falconner, Faulconer and Faulkner.

Farley A variant of Fairleigh.

Farnham English word meaning 'field of ferns'. Variants are Farnam and Farnum.

Farrell Celtic for 'heroic'. Variants are Farrel, Farrill and Ferrell.

Faruq Arabic name, meaning 'honest'. Also Farook, Farooq, Farouk and Faruqh.

Felix Latin for 'fortunate', 'happy'. Other forms of the name are Félice, Feliciano, Felicio, Feliks, Félix and Felizio.

Felton English, meaning 'field town'.

Fenton English, meaning marshland farm.

Ferdinand Old German for 'adventurous life'. The Italian form is Ferdinando, the Polish is Ferdynand, the Spanish Fernando. The French use Ferrand.

Fergus Irish for 'strong', 'manly'. Variants are Fearghas, Feargus, Fergie, Ferguson and Fergusson; the short form is Gus.

Ferguson   Son of Fergus.

Ferris   The Irish form of Peter. Also Farris, Farrish and Ferriss.

Fidel   Latin for 'faithful', 'sincere'. Also Fidele, Fidèle, Fidelis and Fido.

Finlay   Celtic for 'fair-haired hero'. Variants are Findlay, Findley and Finley.

Finn   Celtic for 'fair-haired', a short form of Finlay. In German, Finn refers to someone from Finland.

Firdaus   Indonesian name meaning 'paradise'.

Fitz   The Old English form of the French *fils*, meaning 'son of'. Also a short form of names starting with Fitz.

Fitzgerald   Old English for the 'son of the spear-mighty'.

Fitzroy   Irish for the 'son of Roy'; French for 'son of the king', a surname given to illegitimate children of the king.

Flann   An Irish name meaning 'redhead'. A possible contraction of Flannery.

Fletcher   From the Old English, meaning 'arrow featherer' or 'arrow maker'.

Flint   English, meaning 'a stream' and also 'flintstone'. Sometimes spelt Flynt.

Florian   From the Latin, meaning 'flowering, blooming'. Variants include Florien, Florrian and Floryan.

Floyd   A form of Lloyd.

Flynn   Irish, meaning 'son of the red-haired one'.

Forbes   Irish for 'prosperous' or 'owner of fields'.

Ford   Old English for 'river crossing'.

Forrest   English, meaning 'forest guardian'. Variations are Forrester, Forster and Foster.

Foster   Old French for 'woodsman', sometimes used as a short form of Forester.

Francis   Latin for 'free'. St Francis of Assisi was the

33

founder of the Franciscan order. The Italian form is
Francesco; the Spanish and Portuguese is Francisco
and Franco; the French is François; and Franz is the
German.

Frank, Frankie Diminutives of Francis and Franklin.

Franklin Old English, meaning 'free landholder', a
surname that is also used as a first name. Frank and
Frankie are diminutives.

Franz German form of Francis. Other variants are
Frantz, Franzen and Franzl.

Fraser Old English for 'curly haired' or Old French
for 'strawberry'. Also spelt Frasier, Frazer or Frazier.

Fred A short form of Frederick. See also Alfred and
Manfred.

Freddy, Freddie A familiar form of Frederick.

Frederick From the Old German for 'peaceful ruler'.
The German forms are Friedrich, Fritz and
Fritzchen; the Italian Federico and Federigo; the
Spanish Federico, Fico and Lico; and the English
forms and diminutives are Fred, Freddie, Fredrick,
Rick and Ricky.

Fyodor The Russian form of Theodore.

G

Gabriel From the Hebrew, meaning 'man of God'.
The archangel is mentioned several times in the
Bible, and Gabriel has been in occasional use as a
first name since the Middle Ages. Feminine forms
are Gabriella and Gabrielle. The Hungarian form is
Gabor, the Italian Gabriele and Gabriello and the
Arabic Jibri. Short forms include Gaby and Gabo.

Gaius From the Latin *gaudere*, meaning 'to rejoice'.
Variants are Caius and Kay. See also Jay. The
Italian variant is Gaetano.

Galbraith Irish for 'foreign Briton'. In Ireland the
name would have been used to describe a Scot.

Galen From the Greek for 'healer' or 'tranquil'. A
second-century Greek physician named Claudius
Galen was an authority on the emergent practice
of medicine. Also Gaylen and Gaylin.

Garcia The Spanish form of Gerald.

Gardner A Middle English occupational surname,
meaning 'gardener'. Another variant is Gardiner.

Gareth From the Welsh, meaning 'gentle', and the
name of one of Arthur's knights. Short form is Gary,
and variants include Garry, Garrie and Garith and
Garyth.

Garfield Old English name meaning 'field of spears'.
A surname and a placename.

Garner Middle English name meaning 'to gather
grain'. Quite possibly an occupational surname.

Garnet Originally a surname, from the Old English
for 'spear' and Old French for 'red like a
pomegranate'. Also spelt Garnett.

Garret A variant of Gerard that dates from the
Middle Ages. Other variants include Garrett, Jarret,
Jarrett and Jarrot.

Garrick A name derived from the Old English
surname meaning 'spear' and 'ruler'.

Garrie See Gary.

Garth Of Scandinavian origin, meaning 'enclosure' or
'keeper of the garden'.

Gary, Garry Diminutives of Garret, Garrett and Garrick.

Gaspar Possibly Persian for 'he who guards the
treasure'. A variant of Casper. Other variants
include Kaspar, Kasper, Jasper and Caspar.

Gaston   From the French, meaning 'man from Gascony', a region in the south of France.

Gavin   A Welsh name meaning 'white falcon' or 'little falcon'. Its variant, Gawain, was of the knights of the Round Table, the nephew of King Arthur.

Gawain   See Gavin.

Gaylord   From the Old French, meaning 'high spirited'.

Gene   A short form of Eugene (Greek for 'well-born'), but also used as a name in its own right, for instance Gene Kelly and Gene Hackman.

Geoff, Jeff   Diminutives of Geoffrey.

Geoffrey, Jeffrey, Jeffery   From any of the Old German names Gaufrid, Walahfrid or Gidfrid, derived from the words for 'district', 'traveller' or *frithu*, 'peace'. The name was introduced into Britain from France in the eleventh century. The German form is Gottfried; the Italian Geoffredo and Giotto; the Russian Gottfrid; and the Spanish Godofredo and Godfredo.

Geordie   A pet name for George used in Scotland and northern Britain. Sometimes used as a name in its own right.

George   From the Greek *georgos*, 'tiller of the soil' or 'farmer'. George is the patron saint of England, and the legend of St George and the dragon dates back to the Middle Ages. Its feminine forms are Georgette, Georgia, Georgiana and Georgina. The French form is Georges; the Danish Groer and Joren; the Czechoslovakian form is Jiri, Jurko and Jurik; the German Jurgen, Keorg and Juergen; the Greek Giorgis, Girogos; the Russian Egor and Georgii; the Spanish Jorge and Yoyi; the Swedish and Norwegian Georg and Jorgen.

Geraint   A Welsh variant of the Latin name Gerontius, ultimately from the Greek *geron*, 'old'. A Sir Geraint figures in Arthurian legends, the husband of Enid.

Gerald From the Old German name meaning 'spear' and 'rule'. Diminutives are Gerry and Jerry. The feminine form is Geraldine. The French form is Geraud, Giraud and Girauld; the Italian and Spanish Geraldo.

Gerard From the Old German name derived from *ger* 'spear' and *hardu* 'bold'. Variants are Garret and Garrett, and it shares the same diminutives as Gerald. The French form is Gérard.

Germaine French for 'from Germany'. Among its many variants are Germain, Germane and Jermaine.

Gerontius See Geraint.

Gerry, Jerry Diminutives of Gerald, Geraldine and Gerard. Jerry is also a diminutive of Jeremiah, Jeremy and Jerome.

Gershom From the Hebrew, meaning 'alien' or 'bell', an Old Testament name that appears in Exodus. Also Gersham, Gershon and Gerson.

Gervaise, Gervase From an Old German name derived from *ger* 'spear' and a Celtic word meaning 'servant'. Jarvey, Jarvis and Jervis are variants.

Gerwyn A Welsh name, meaning 'fair love'.

Giacomo An Italian variation of Jacob.

Gibson Old English, meaning 'son of Gilbert'. Short forms and variants are Gibb, Gibbons and Gilson.

Gideon From the Hebrew, meaning 'feller of trees'. It is the name of a biblical judge who, with an army of 300 men, liberated the Israelis from the Midianites.

Gilbert From the Old German name Gisilbert, meaning 'pledge' and 'bright', introduced into Britain at the time of the Norman Conquest. Short forms are Gob and Gil; the feminine forms are Gilberta and Gilbertine.

Giles From the Greek, meaning 'young goat'. St Giles was the patron saint of beggars. The Scottish Gaelic form is Gillies, and the French is Gilles.

Gilroy   Celtic, meaning 'servant of the red-haired man'. Gil is a diminutive.

Giorgio   An Italian form of George.

Giovanni   The Italian form of John.

Giuseppe   Italian form of Joseph.

Glanville   From an Old French word, meaning 'settlement of oak trees'.

Glen, Glenn   Derived from the Gaelic *gleann*, 'valley'. Variants are Glyn and Glynn.

Glyn   The Welsh form of Glen.

Godfrey   From the Old German name Godafrid, meaning 'god' and 'peace', introduced into Britain at the time of the Norman conquest.

Godwin   From the Old English name Godwine, a compound of *god* 'god' and *wine* 'friend'.

Goldsworthy   Old English for 'God's enclosure'.

Gordon   A Scottish surname of uncertain meaning, possibly a placename meaning 'hill near meadows' or 'triangular hill'.

Gorej   The Slavonic form of Gregory.

Gough   Welsh for 'red-haired'.

Graham, Grahame, Graeme   From a Scottish surname derived from the placename Grantham; ultimately from the Old English meaning 'Granta's homestead'.

Grant   A Scottish surname derived from the French *grand*, meaning 'tall'.

Grantley   A variant of Grant.

Granville   From a surname derived from a French placename, meaning 'big town'. Grenville is a variant.

Greg   Diminutive of Gregory, sometimes used as an independent name.

Gregor   A variant of Gregory, and also the German form of Gregory.

Gregory   From the Greek, meaning 'watchful', a name borne by numerous popes and saints. Variants include Greig, Gregg, Grigor and Gregorio.

Gresham   An Old English placename, meaning 'village surrounded by pasture'.

Griffith   From the Welsh name Gruffudd or Gruffydd, probably meaning 'strong chief'. Used as both a surname and a first name, as Griffiths or Griffin.

Grover   From an Old English surname, meaning 'grove dweller'.

Guillaume   French form of William.

Guntar   See Gunther.

Gunther   From the Old German for 'battle army'. Other variants are Gunnar and Guntar.

Gus   A diminutive of Augustine or Augustus and sometimes Gustav. Also a name in its own right.

Gustav, Gustave   From the Swedish name Gustaf, meaning 'staff of the gods'. The latinised form is Gustavus. Gustave is the French form. Also spelt Gustaf.

Guthrie   From the Irish placename, meaning 'windy spot'.

Guy   From the Latin for 'life' or Old German for 'warrior'. The Italian and Spanish form is Guido.

Gwilym, Gwylim   Welsh variants of William.

Gyles   See Giles.

Hadden, Haddon   Derived from an Old English placename, meaning 'hill of heather'. Also Haden and Hadon.

Hadrian   A variant of Adrian.

Hakim   Arabic name meaning 'wise' or 'ruler'.

Hal   A diminutive of Harold, Harry or Henry, sometimes used as an independent name.

Haley   From an Old English placename for 'hay meadow' or the Irish for 'ingenious, clever'. Variants are Hailey, Haleigh and Hayley. Hayley is usually used as a girls' name.

Halford   Derived from an Old English placename, meaning 'valley ford'.

Hall   An occupational name denoting 'worker at the hall', usually a large house or manor.

Hallam   From the Old Norse, meaning 'from the rocks'.

Hamilton   From a Scottish surname and placename, meaning 'hill with grass' or 'fortified castle'.

Hamish   The Scottish form of James, from the Gaelic Seumas (see Seamus).

Hamlet   From the Old German or French meaning 'village, home'. The name is derived from the German root that means 'home'. Hamlet is also the name of Shakespeare's Danish prince.

Hanif   An Arabic name meaning 'true believer'.

Hank   A diminutive of Henry of Dutch origin, sometimes used as an independent name.

Hans   The German form of John. Also spelt Hanns.

Hardy   From the Old German surname meaning 'bold' or 'brave'.

Harlan   Derived from an Old English placename, meaning 'army land'. Variants include Harland, Harlen, Harlin and Harlyn.

Harley   From a surname and a placename, meaning 'hare wood or pasture'. Its diminutives and variants are Arlea, Arley, Harlee and Harleigh.

Harold   From the Old English name Hereweald, meaning 'army' and 'power'. Its English diminutives

are Harry and Hal. The French form is Arry; the
Hungarian Henrik; the Italian Araldo, Aroldo and
Arrigo; the Danish and Swede form is Harald; and
the Spanish Haraldo. See also Errol.

Haroun The Arabic form of Aaron, 'lofty' or 'exalted'.

Harper From the Old English, meaning 'harp player'.

Harris The Old English for 'Harry's son'.

Harrison From a surname meaning 'Harry's son'.

Harry Originally a variant of Henry, but since the
Middle Ages has been used as a diminutive of
Harold and also as a name in its own right. Its
diminutive is Hal and the feminine form Harriet.

Hartley From the Old English surname and
placename, meaning 'stag wood' or 'meadow'.
Variants are Hartlea, Hartlee and Hartleigh.

Harvey From the French Hervé, derived from the
Celtic words for 'battle' or 'strong' and 'worthy' and
'ardent'. The name was borne by a Breton saint of
the sixth century. Hervey is a variant.

Hassan An Arabic name meaning 'handsome'.

Hayden, Haydn, Haydon From a surname and
placename of uncertain origin, but believed to mean
'hedged valley'. It may have been influenced by the
Celtic name Aidan.

Heath From the English word, meaning 'heath or
field of heather'. Heather is the feminine form.

Heathcliff A Middle English name indicating a cliff
near a heath. The name is also associated with the
hero of Emily Brontë's *Wuthering Heights*.

Hector From the Greek, meaning 'holding fast', a
name borne in Greek mythology by one of the
warriors of the Trojan War. The verb 'hector',
however, means to bully or browbeat.

Heinrich The German diminutive of Henry.

Helmut From the German, meaning 'famous courage'.

Henderson   Old English, meaning 'son of Henry'.

Henley   From an Old English placename, meaning 'high meadow'. A variant of Hanley.

Henri   The French form of Henry.

Henrik   The Swedish form of Henry.

Henry   From the Old German name Haimrich, meaning 'home ruler'. In the Latin it means 'a person of high rank'. The feminine form is Henrietta, the variant Harry, and the diminutives Hal, Hank and Hen. Among its other variants are Arrigo, Enrico and Enzio (Italian); Enrique and Quinto (Spanish); Heinz and Heine (German) and Hersz (Yiddish).

Herb   Often used as a diminutive of Herbert.

Herbert   From an Old German name derived from *harja* 'army' and *berhta* 'bright'. Its diminutives are Herb, Bert, Bertie and Herbie.

Herman, Hermann   From the Old German name Hariman, meaning 'army' and 'man' – 'warrior'. Its variants are Armand, Armando, Armant, Ermanno and Hermano. The feminine forms are Armina and Armine.

Herrick   From the Old German, meaning 'war ruler'. Also Herryck.

Hervé   See Harvey.

Heywood   From the Old English, 'from the hedged forest'. Also Haywood.

Hilary, Hillary   Both a male and female name, from the Latin name Hilarius, derived from *hilaris* 'cheerful'. The French form is Hilaire. Variant is Ellery.

Hiram   From the Hebrew, of slightly obscured meaning, but possibly 'God is high'.

Ho   Chinese for 'river'.

Holden   From a surname and placename, an Old English name meaning 'hollow valley'.

Holmes   From the Old Norse, meaning 'river flat'.

Homer   From the Greek, meaning 'security, pledge'. The name of the epic poet and author of the *Iliad* and the *Odyssey*.

Horace   From the Roman clan name Horatius, possibly meaning 'timekeeper'. Borne in the first century BC by the Roman poet of the same name. Used as a name in its own right and as a diminutive of Horatio. The feminine equivalent is Horatia.

Horatio   A form of Horatius, a Latin family name. See also Horace.

Howard   Of disputed origins, but possibly from the Old German name Huguard, *hugu* 'heart' and *vardu* 'protection' or *hardu* 'bold', or from the Old English words for 'hog-warden' or 'fence guardian'.

Howell   Welsh for 'eminent'. The anglicised form of Hywel.

Hubert   From the Old German name Hugubert, meaning 'heart' and 'bright'. Short forms are Bert and Hube; Hobart is a variant.

Hudson   Meaning 'son of Richard'.

Hugh, Hew   From an Old German name meaning 'heart, mind'. Huw, a Welsh spelling of the name, may be derived from a Celtic word for 'fire' or 'inspiration'. Short forms and variants include Huey, Hughes, Hughie and Hugo.

Hugo   The Latin form of Hugh.

Humphrey   From the Old English name Hunfrith, probably derived from the words for 'giant' and 'peace'. Hunfrid is the Old German equivalent of the name, introduced to Britain at the time of the Norman Conquest. Variant spellings and forms include Humphry, Onofredo and Onofrio.

Hurley   Old English for 'wood clearing'.

Hyman   An anglicised form of Chaim, probably from

a Hebrew word for 'life'. Diminutives include Hy
and Hymie; a variant is Hyam.

Hywel   From the Welsh *hywe*, meaning 'eminent'.
Howell and Howel are anglicised versions of the
name.

I

Iago   A Spanish form of James. In the Hebrew it
means 'he who supplants', but it is generally
associated with the villain of Shakespeare's *Othello*.

Iain   The Scottish form of Ian.

Ian   The anglicised, Scottish form of John, meaning
'God is gracious'. Variants are Ean and Eann.

Ibn   Arabic for 'son of'.

Ibrahim   The Arabic form of Abraham, meaning
'father of many'.

Ignatius   Of uncertain origin, though sometimes
associated with the Latin *igneus*, 'fire'. The short
form is Iggy. The Spanish form is Ignacio, the
German Ignaz.

Igor   The Russian form of the Scandinavian name
Ingvar, meaning 'Ing's warrior', Ing being one of
the Norse gods of peace and fertility.

Ike   Diminutive of Isaac.

Ilya   The Russian form of Elias, 'Jehovah is God'.

Immanuel   A form of Emmanuel.

Imran   Muslim name meaning 'strong'.

Imre   A Hungarian name.

Ingmar   From the Old Norse, meaning 'famous son'.
Variants include Ingemar.

Ingram   From the Old German name Ingilramnus,

probably meaning 'Ing's raven' (see Igor). Used as both a surname and first name.

Inigo   The Greek form of Ignatius.

Ion   A form of John, used by the Australian author Ion Idriess.

Ira   Hebrew for 'watchful', borne in the Old Testament by one of King David's men.

Irvin   Both a surname and a Scottish placename. Also a form of Irving.

Irving   Old English for 'sea friend'. Used as both a first name and surname. The variations are Irvin and Irvine.

Irwin   From the Old English meaning 'boar friend'. Used as both a first name and surname.

Isaac   From the Hebrew, meaning 'he laughs', given by Abraham and Sarah to the son born in their old age. Diminutives are Ike, Zack and Zac. The Bulgarian, Russian and Norwegian form is Isak, and the German and Greek is Isaak. The Yiddish form is Yitzhak.

Isaiah   From the Hebrew, meaning 'the Lord is generous'.

Iskandar   The Turkish form of Alexander.

Ismail   The Arabic form of Samuel, also the name of a Muslim prophet.

Israel   From the Hebrew, possibly meaning 'struggling with God', after Jacob's three-day bout with the Lord. Also the name of the Jewish republic created in 1948.

Ivan   The Russian form of John, 'gracious gift of God'.

Ives   Old English for 'son of the yew bough' or 'little archer'.

Ivo   From the Old German, meaning 'yew'. See also Ivor. Variants are Ives and Yves; the feminine forms are Yvette and Yvonne.

Ivor From the Norse, but the meaning is unclear, and possibly related to Ivo.

Izaak See Isaac.

Izzy A diminutive of many masculine and feminine names beginning with Is, such as Isaac, Isabel or Isadore.

J

Jabez From the Hebrew, possibly meaning 'borne in pain'. The name was adopted by the Puritans in the seventeenth century and was quite often used in the nineteenth century.

Jabir An Arabic name, meaning 'consolation'.

Jack A diminutive of John, derived from the Hebrew, meaning 'god is gracious'. It is also used as a colloquial word for 'man' and 'boy'. Diminutives include Jackie and Jacky.

Jackson The surname 'son of Jack', used as a first name and surname.

Jacob From the Hebrew, meaning 'supplanter'. The Jacob of the Old Testament was the younger son of Isaac. Jake is the diminutive and its feminine equivalents Jacoba and Jacobina. Among its English forms are Jakob, Jamie, James, Jay, Jayme, Jimmie and Jamison. The Czechoslovakian forms are Jakub and Jokubas; the Dutch is Jaap; the French Jacques and Jacque; the German Jakob and Jocek; the Irish Seamus; the Italian Iago, Giacomo; the Latin Jacobus; and the Spanish Jaime, Santiago, Diego, Diaz and Jacobo.

Jacques The French form of James through Jacob.

Feminine forms are Jacqueline and Jacquelyn.

Jago   A Cornish variant of Jacob.

Jaime   A spelling variant of James, also Jaimie, Jayme and Jaymie.

Jake   A diminutive of Jacob, also used as a name in its own right.

Jamal   Arabic for 'handsome'. Also Jamahl, Jameel, Jamil and Jammal.

James   From the same root as Jacob (Hebrew for 'supplanter'), derived from Jacomus. James was the name of two of Jesus' apostles: St James the Great, son of Zebedee and brother of St John, and St James the Less. Its variants are Hamish, Seamus and Shamus; diminutives Jamie, Jim and Jimmy.

Jamie   A familiar form of James.

Jamieson   'Son of Jamie'. Spelling variants include Jameson and Jamison.

Jan   The Dutch variant of John. Other variants are Hans, Janek and Janos.

Jared   From the Hebrew, possibly meaning 'he descends'. An Old Testament name used by the Puritans. Spelling variants include Jarred, Jarret, Jarrett and Jarrod.

Jarrett   See Jared.

Jarvis   A variant of Gervaise.

Jason, Jayson   The Greek form of a Hebrew name, possibly meaning 'healer'. Borne in Greek mythology by the leader of the Argonauts and in the New Testament.

Jasper   The English form of Casper, possibly from the Persian meaning 'he who guards the treasure'. Jasper is also a type of quartz.

Javan   From the Hebrew, meaning 'clay', or pertaining to the Indonesian island of Java.

Jay   From the bird name, which may be ultimately

derived from the Latin Gaius. Also used as a
diminutive of any masculine and feminine name
beginning with 'J'.

Jean   The French form of John, also a girls' name.

Jeff   Diminutive of Jeffrey.

Jefferson   'Son of Geoffrey', used as both a surname
and a first name.

Jeffrey   An alternate form of Geoffrey, meaning 'peace'.

Jeremiah   From the Hebrew, meaning 'may Jehovah
exalt'. The Jeremiah of the Old Testament was a
prophet of the seventh century BC. Its diminutive is
Jerry, and variant, Jeremy.

Jeremy   The English form of Jeremiah, which dates
back to the thirteenth century. See Jeremiah.

Jermaine   From the French name Germain, meaning
'German'. The feminine form is Germaine.

Jerome   From the Greek, meaning 'blessed name' or
'calling'. Jerome is the patron saint of archaeologists
and scholars. Variants include Hieronymus,
Jeronimo, Geronimo, Herry and Gerry.

Jerry   A short form of Gerald, Jeremiah, Jeremy and
Jerome.

Jervis   A form of Gerald.

Jesse, Jessie, Jessey   Hebrew for 'Jehovah is'. The name
borne by the father of King David.

Jethro   From the Hebrew, meaning 'excellence'. The
name of the father-in-law of Moses in the Bible.

Jibri   Arabic for the 'archangel', a form of Gabriel.

Jim, Jimmy, Jimmie   Diminutives of James, sometimes
used as independent names.

Joachim   From the Hebrew, meaning 'may Jehovah
exalt'. The name of the Virgin Mary's father.
Variants and diminutives are Achim, Akim, Joakim
and Joaquin.

Jock   The Scottish diminutive of John.

Joe Diminutive of Joseph, also used as a name in its own right.

Joel Either from the Hebrew, meaning 'Jehovah is God' or from the name of a Breton saint. Joel was a fifth-century BC prophet of the Old Testament.

Joey A diminutive of Joseph, sometimes used as a name in its own right. In Australia 'joey' refers to a young kangaroo.

Johann, Johannes German forms of John.

John From the Hebrew, meaning 'Jehovah is gracious' or 'Jehovah has favoured'. There are two New Testament bearers: St John the Baptist and St John the Divine. Its diminutives are Jack, Jock, Johnnie or Johnny. The feminine forms are Jane, Janet, Janice, Janis, Jayne, Jean, Jeanne, Joan, Joanna, Joanne and Shona. It has many variants, and what follows is by no means comprehensive: Jan (Belgian); Ivan (Bulgarian); Janek, Jano and Jenda (Czechoslovakian); Hans, Jan (Danish); Johan (Estonian); Jean and Jeannot (French); Hans, Hansel, Johann, Johannes (German); Giannes, Giannis, Giannos and Ioannes (Greek); Sean, Seann, Shane (Irish); Giovanni, Gianetto (Italian); Vanya, Vanko, Yanka (Russian); Ian (Scottish); Juan, Juanito and Juancho (Spanish); Hans, Hasse (Swedish); Evan (Welsh) and Yochanan (Yiddish).

Johnson 'Son of John'. Variants include Jonson and Johnston.

Jonah From the Hebrew, meaning 'dove'. Jonah was the biblical hero swallowed alive by a whale, and lived in its belly for three days. Jonas is a variant. The Italian form is Guiseppe.

Jonathan From the Hebrew, meaning 'gift of Jehovah'. In the Old Testament Jonathan was the friend of King David. Jonathan Swift wrote the satire *Gulliver's Travels*. Diminutives and variants include Jon, Jonathon, Johnathan.

Jordan   From the Hebrew, meaning 'flowing down', also the name of a river in the Middle East. Its diminutive is Judd. Variants include Giordano (Italian); Jourdan, Jourdain (French); and Jared (Hebrew).

Jorge   The Spanish form of George.

José   The Spanish form of Joseph.

Josef   The Polish German form of Joseph.

Joseph   From the Hebrew, meaning 'Jehovah has added', referring to an increase in the size of the family. The husband of Mary in the Bible. Its diminutives are Joe and Joey. Feminine forms include Josepha, Josephine, Josette and Pepita. Among its variants are Josef, Jozef and Pepa (Czechoslovakian); Josephe (French); Beppi, Peppi and Josef (German); Guiseppe, Pino (Italian); Jo (Japan); Jose (Portuguese); Che, Pepe, Pepin (Spanish); and Yousef (Yiddish).

Josh   A diminutive of Joshua.

Joshua   From the Hebrew, meaning 'Jehovah is generous'. The Joshua of the Old Testament led the Israelites to the Promised Land and made the walls of Jericho fall. Its diminutive is Josh, and among its variants are Giosia (Italian); Joaquin and Josue (Spanish); and Yehosha (Yiddish).

Juan   The Spanish form of John.

Judah   From the Hebrew, possibly meaning 'to praise'. Judah was the fourth son of Jacob and Leah. Variants are Judas, Jude and Yehudi.

Jud, Judd   Diminutives of Judah, Judas and Jordan.

Jude   A variant of Judah. St Jude was one of Jesus Christ's apostles, also known as Judas or Thaddaeus.

Jules The French form of Julius. See Julius.

Julian From the Latin name Julianus, derived from Julius. Feminine forms are Gillian, Jillian, Juliana, Julianne and Julienne. The French form is Julien; the Spanish Julio.

Julius From the clan name, meaning 'young' or 'fair bearded'. The most famous clan member was Julius Caesar.

Justin From the Latin for 'just'. Justinian was the Roman emperor of the East. Its feminine forms are Justine and Justina. Among its variants are Jusa and Justyn (Czechoslovakian); Just and Justus (German); Guistino (Italian); Justyn (Polish); Justino and Justo (Spanish); and Justinus (Swedish and Norwegian).

K

Kalil From the Arabic, meaning 'friend'. Also spelt Kahlil and Khalil.

Kamil From the Arabic, meaning 'without peer'. Also Kameel.

Kane From a surname of uncertain origin; possibly Welsh for 'beautiful' or from the French placename Caen, meaning 'place of combat' or from the Celtic word for warrior. Not related to the Cain in the Bible.

Karel The Bohemian, Dutch, Swedish and Estonian form of Charles.

Karl The German form of Charles. See also Carl.

Kazuo From the Japanese, meaning 'man of peace'.

Keefe From the Irish Gaelic, meaning 'attractive' or

'beloved'. Also Keifer and Keefer.

Keenan From the Irish Gaelic, meaning 'little ancient one'. Its variants are Kienan, Kienen and Kynan.

Keiran See Kieran.

Keith From a Scottish surname and placename, possibly meaning 'wood'.

Kel A diminutive of Kelvin.

Kelsey From an Old English placename, possibly meaning 'island'. Also Kelsie and Kelsy, a name used for both boys and girls.

Kelvin A name of uncertain origin, possibly derived from the Old English words meaning 'ship' and 'friend'. Variants and diminutives include Kel, Kell, Kelvyn, Kelwin and Kelwyn.

Ken A diminutive of Kenneth, Kennedy and other names with 'Ken' such as McKenzie.

Kendall From a surname and placename, meaning 'valley of the River Kent'. Also Kendal, Kendell and Kenny.

Kennedy From the Irish Gaelic, meaning 'ugly helmet'. A well-known surname also used as a first or second name.

Kenneth From the Gaelic, meaning 'handsome', also the name of the first king of Scotland. English variants include Kennett, Kennith and Kenney; the Russian is Kenya and Kesha; the Spanish Chencho, Incencio and Inocente.

Kenny A diminutive of Kenneth.

Kenrick Either from the Old English name Cynric, meaning 'royal ruler', or from the Welsh, meaning 'chief hero'.

Kent The name of a county in England. Used as both a first name and surname.

Kenton Old English, 'from the royal manor'. Used as both a first name and surname.

Kerr From the Irish Gaelic, meaning 'sword' or 'black' or 'spear'.

Kerry From the name of an Irish county, from the Irish Gaelic meaning 'descendants of Ciar', also 'dark-haired child'. Used more often for girls. Also Kerrie and Kerrey.

Kerwin Possibly Old English for 'swamp friend' or Irish Gaelic for 'little dark one'. Variants are Kervin, Kervyn and Kerwinn.

Kevin From an Irish Gaelic name meaning 'handsome'. St Kevin was one of the patron saints of Dublin. Variants are Kevan, Keven and Kevyn. Kev is the short form.

Kieran From the Irish name Ciaran, meaning 'dark'. The name was borne by two Irish saints of the fifth and sixth centuries. Variants include Keiran, Kernan, Kiernan and Kieron.

Kiernan See Kieran.

Kilian Irish, meaning 'strife'. Also Keelan, Killian and Killin.

Kim A diminutive of Kimball or Kimberly, also used as a name in its own right. Kim is Vietnamese and Chinese for 'gold'.

Kimball From the Old English, meaning 'bold war-leader'. Also Kimbal, Kimbell and Kimble.

Kimberly, Kimberley From a surname and placename meaning 'wood'. Usually associated with a South African city. The full form Kimberly has been taken over by girls.

Kingsley From an Old English surname and placename, meaning 'king's wood or meadow'.

Kingston From the Old English, meaning 'out of the kingdom'.

Kirby From the Old Norse, meaning 'church farm or village'.

Kirk   From a surname derived from the Old Norse *kirkja*, 'church'.

Kit   A diminutive of Christopher.

Klaus   A variant of Claus, diminutive of Nicholas. Also spelt Claus. See Nicholas.

Konrad   The German and Swedish form of Conrad.

Kris   A form of Chris. See Christopher.

Krishna   From the Hindi, meaning 'pleasurable' or 'inspiring'.

Kristian   The Danish form of Christian.

Kristofer   The Scandinavian form of Christopher.

Kurt   The German variant of Conrad (also Curt). Kurt Weill was a German composer.

Kyle   From a surname derived from a Scottish word for 'strait' or 'channel'.

Kyrin   The Scottish form of Kieran.

L

Laban   From the Hebrew, meaning 'white'. Laban was Rebekah's brother in the Old Testament.

Lachlan   From the Scottish Gaelic, meaning either 'warlike' or 'fjords land', a reference to Scandinavia or the Vikings. Also Lachlann, Lochlan and Loughlin.

Lambert   From an Old German name derived from *landa*, meaning 'land' and *berhta*, 'bright'. St Lambert was a seventh-century bishop and martyr.

Lance   A name of French origin, ultimately from the Old German *landa*, meaning 'land'. A diminutive of Lancelot.

Lancelot   From the Old French, meaning 'servant'.
The name is generally associated with one of King
Arthur's knights of the Round Table.

Lane   A Middle English placename. Also Laine.

Lang   From the Old Norse, meaning 'tall one'. Also
Lange.

Larry   A diminutive of Laurence or Lawrence.

Lars   The Scandinavian form of Lawrence.

Latif   From the Arabic for 'pleasant', 'gentle'. Also
spelt Lateef.

Latimer   From the Old French, meaning 'teacher of
Latin'.

Laurent   The French form of Laurence.

Laurence, Lawrence   From the Latin Laurentius, 'of
Laurentum', an ancient Italian town famed for its
laurel groves. St Laurence was a third-century
martyr. Its diminutives are Larry, Laurie and Lawrie.
Laurencia and Laurentia are feminine forms. Among
its variants are Lauritz and Lorenz (Danish); Laurens
(Dutch); Lauri (Finnish); Laurent (French); Lorenz
(German and Polish); Lorenzo and Renzo (Italian);
Lourenco (Portuguese); Lavr and Lavro (Russian);
and Laurencio, Lorenzo (Spanish); Lars, Larse and
Loren (Swedish and Norwegian).

Laurie   A Scottish diminutive of Laurence, also a
name in its own right. Also spelt Lawrie.

Lawson   Old English for 'son of Lawrence'.

Lawton   Old English placename, meaning 'hill town'.

Layton, Leighton   From an Old English surname and
placename, meaning 'herb garden'.

Lee   From an Old English placename, meaning
'pasture' or 'meadow'. A name used by both boys
and girls. Also Leigh.

Leif   Scandinavian, meaning 'loved'.

Leighton   See Layton.

Leith From the Scottish Gaelic, meaning 'broad river'.

Leland From an Old English placename, meaning 'meadow land'. Also Leyland.

Lemuel From the Hebrew, meaning 'devoted to God', the name of an Old Testament king and Gulliver, the hero of Jonathan Swift's satire. Its diminutive is Lemmy.

Len A diminutive of Leonard.

Lenny, Lennie Diminutives of Leonard.

Lennox From a Scottish surname and placename, meaning 'people of the lake Leven'. A surname also used as a first name.

Leo From the Latin *leo*, meaning 'lion'. The fifth-century pope and twelve of his successors bore the name. Variants include Leon, Lee and Lyon.

Leon From the Greek *leon*, meaning 'lion', a variant of Leo. The feminine forms are Leona and Leonie. See also Lionel.

Leonard From the Old German name Leonhard, derived from *levon* 'lion' and *hardu* 'hardy'.
St Leonard was the patron saint of prisoners. Its diminutives are Lee, Len, Lenard, Lenn, Lennie, Lenny, Leo, Leon and Lonny. The French form is Lienard; the German Leonhard; the Italian, Portuguese and Spanish Leonardo; the Lithuanian Leonards; the Polish Leonek, Linek and Nardek; and the Russian Lonya and Leonid.

Leopold From the Old German *leudi* 'people' and *balda* 'bold'. Leo is a diminutive.

Leroy From a surname derived from the Old French, meaning 'the king'. Variants are Elroy, Lee and Roy.

Les A diminutive of Lesley, Leslie or Lester.

Leslie From a Gaelic placename, meaning 'grey

castle'. The spelling Lesley is used almost exclusively in the feminine sense; Leslie is the masculine form of the name. Les is a diminutive for both.

Lester From a surname, possibly derived from the English placename Leicester. Short form is Les.

Levi From the Hebrew, meaning 'attached' or 'pledged'. Levi was one of the sons of Jacob and Leah in the Old Testament.

Lew A diminutive of Lewis.

Lewis An anglicised form of the French Louis. Lewis was sometimes used in place of Llewellyn.

Lex A diminutive of Alexander.

Leyland A variant of Leland.

Liam The Irish variant of William.

Lincoln A name derived from the English placename Lincoln, meaning 'Roman colony at the pool'. Abraham Lincoln was an American president.

Lindley From the Old English, meaning 'linden tree meadow'. Also Lindlea, Lindlee and Lindleigh.

Lindsay, Lindsey From a Scottish surname and English placename, meaning 'island of linden trees'. Also popular as a girls' name. Variants include Lindsey, Linsey, Lyndsay and Lyndsey.

Linford From an Old English placename, meaning 'linden tree ford' or 'flax ford'.

Linley From the Old English placename, meaning 'flax meadow'. Also Linlea, Linlee and Linleigh.

Linton From the Old English, meaning 'flax meadow'.

Linus From the Greek, meaning 'flax', often in reference to someone who is flaxen or fair-haired.

Lionel A diminutive of Leon or its medieval variant Lyon, meaning 'young lion'. One of the knights of King Arthur's Round Table. The Spanish form is Lionello, Leonel, Lionell and Lonnell.

Llewellyn, Llewelyn From the Welsh name Llywelyn, derived from *llyw*, meaning 'leader' or 'lion'. Its short form is Lew.

Lloyd From the Welsh *llwyd*, meaning 'grey', used as both a first name and as a surname. A variant is Floyd.

Llywelyn See Llewellyn.

Logan From the Irish Gaelic, meaning 'small cove'.

Loren, Lauren, Lorin Variants of Laurence.

Lorenzo The Spanish and Italian form of Laurence.

Lorimer From the Latin, meaning 'one who makes harnesses'.

Lorne The name of an early Scottish chieftain, which subsequently became a placename. Used for both boys and girls.

Lou A diminutive of Louis, Louisa or Louise.

Louis From the Old German or Old French, meaning 'famous warrior'. Louis was used by the French royal family and was borne by eighteen kings. The anglicised form is Lewis, and other variants are Aloysius, Louie, Ludvig and Ludovic. The feminine forms are Louisa and Louise; the diminutives Lou and Louie.

Lovell From the Old French, meaning 'old cub'. Lowell, Lowe and Lowel are variants.

Lucas The latinised form of Luke.

Lucian From the Latin name Lucianus, possibly meaning 'illumination'. Its French variants are Lucien and Lucianus; the Italian Lucio, Luciano, Lucan and Lucca. The feminine forms are Luciana and Lucienne.

Lucio The Italian form of Lucian.

Lucius From the Latin, meaning 'illumination'. Short forms and variants are Luca, Lucas, Luce, Lucias, Lucio, Lukas and Luke.

Ludovic A variant of Louis, from the latinised form of the name. The diminutive is Ludo.

Ludwig From the German, meaning 'famous victories'.

Luis The Spanish form of Louis.

Luke From the Latin, meaning 'bringer of light' and 'bringer of knowledge'. The English variants are Lucas, Lucian, Lucien; the Czechoslovakian and German Lukas; the French Luce, Lucien and Lucius; the Greek Loukas; the Hungarian Lukacs; the Portuguese and Spanish Lucas; and the Swedish Lukas.

Luther From the German surname, meaning 'warrior' or the Old French for 'lute player'.

Lyall, Lyell, Lyle Derived from the Old French *l'ile*, meaning 'the island'. Variants Lyall, Lyell and Ly.

Lyndon From the Old English, meaning 'from the hill of linden trees'. Variants are Lyndell, Lindon, Lyn, Lin, Lynn, Linden and Lynden.

Lyndsay See Lindsay.

Mac From the Scottish Gaelic, for 'son of' or 'heir to'. Also a diminutive for names starting with 'Mac'.

Macaulay From the Scottish, meaning 'son of righteousness'.

Macdonald From the Scottish Gaelic, meaning 'Donald's son'. Also MacDonald and McDonald.

Mackenzie From the Irish Gaelic, meaning 'son of the learned leader'. Also MacKenzie and McKenzie.

Madison From the Old English, meaning 'son of the brave soldier'.

Magnus From the Latin *magnus*, meaning 'great'.
The name was borne by a few Scandinavian kings.
Manus is a variant.

Mahmoud A form of Muhammad. Also spelt
Mahmud.

Malachi From the Hebrew, meaning 'my messenger'.
Malachi wrote the last book of the Old Testament.
Its variants are Malachy, Malachie and Malechy.

Malcolm From the Gaelic, meaning 'follower of
St Columbus'. Variants include Callum and Calum.
Famous bearers include Malcolm X (born Malcolm
Little).

Maldwyn The Welsh form of Baldwin.

Malik From the Arabic, meaning 'master'.

Mallory From the Old French, meaning 'without
fortune' or the Old German, 'army counsellor'.
Variants are Mallery, Mallorie, Malory and Mal.

Maloney From the Irish Gaelic, meaning 'church-
going'. Variants are Malone and Malony.

Manfred From an Old German name derived from
mana, meaning 'man' and *frithu*, 'peace'. Diminutive
variants include Manny, Fred and Freddie.

Manley Derived from an English surname, meaning
'manly'.

Manning From the Old English, meaning 'son of a
man'. Manning Clark was an Australian historian.

Manny A diminutive of Emmanuel or Manuel.

Manolis The Greek form of Emmanuel.

Mansel, Mansell From a surname, probably derived
from the French placename Le Mans.

Mansfield From the Old English, meaning 'field by
the narrow waters'.

Manuel A variant of Emmanuel, now used as the
Spanish form of the name. The diminutive is
Manny, and the feminine form Manuela.

Manus From the Gaelic variant of Magnus, which gave rise to the Irish surname McManus.

Marc The French form of Marcus, sometimes used as an alternative spelling of Mark.

Marcel The French form of Marcellus.

Marcellus From the Latin for 'young fighter'. A diminutive of Marcus. Marcel is a variant, and the feminine form is Marcella.

Marco The Italian form of Marcus.

Marcus A Latin name, derived from Mars, the god of war, and therefore meaning 'warlike'. Marcus Antonius, better known as Mark Antony, was a Roman triumvir. Its variants include Marc, Marco. and Mark.

Mario Italian variant of Mark and Marius.

Marius From a Roman clan name derived from Mars, the Roman god of war. Mario is a variant.

Mark A Latin family name, meaning 'warlike'. St Mark was one of Evangelists. The many forms and variants include: Markus (Danish, Dutch, German, Swedish); Marc (French); Marinos and Markos (Greek); Marco (Italian); Marcos (Portuguese and Spanish); and Markusha (Russian).

Marlon From the Old French, meaning 'little hawk'.

Marlow From the Old English, a placename, meaning 'hill near the lake'. Also Marlowe.

Marshall An Old French occupational surname, meaning 'horse-keeper'. Also a military title. The variants and diminutives include Marsh, Marshal and Marshell.

Martin From the Latin name Martinus, derived from Martius, 'of Mars, the Roman god of war' or 'warlike'. The fourth-century St Martin is the patron saint of beggars. Its diminutive is Marty and its feminine forms are Martina and Martine. The

French form is Mertin; the German Martel; the
Greek Martinos; the Hungarian Martino and Marci;
the Italian Martino; the Latvian Martins; the Russian
Martyn; and the Spanish Martianiano.

Marty Diminutive of Martin.

Marvin A name of uncertain origin, possibly from the
Old English meaning 'sea lover'. Among its variants
are Marwin, Mervin, Mervyn, Merwin, Merwyb and
Murvin.

Mason An Old French occupational name meaning
'stone worker'.

Mat, Matt Diminutives of Matthew.

Mathew, Matthew From the Hebrew name Mattathiah,
meaning 'gift of the Lord'. St Matthew was the author
of the first gospel. The Bulgarian form is Matei; the
French Mathieu and Matthieu; the German Matthaus
and Matthias; the Greek Matthaios; the Italian
Matteo; the Norwegian Matteus; the Polish Matyas;
the Portuguese Mateus and the Spanish Matias.
Diminutives are Mat and Matt.

Maurice From the Latin name Mauritius, meaning
'Moorish or dark-skinned'. Morris is the anglicised
form. Other variants are Morice, Maurizio, Mauricio,
Moss, Morrison and Morrisson.

Max Diminutive of Maximilian or Maxwell, often
used as a name in its own right. The feminine form
is Maxine.

Maximilian From the Latin *maximus*, meaning
'greatest'. Its short forms are Mac, Mack, Max,
Maxy. The French is Maxime; the German
Maximalian; the Italian Massimo; the Portuguese
Maximiliano; the Russian Naksim; and the Spanish
Maximino and Maximiliano.

Maxwell From a Scottish surname and placename,
possibly 'Magnus's well'.

Maynard   From the Old German Maganhard,
   meaning 'hard strength'. The name was introduced
   into Britain at the time of the Norman Conquest,
   and is more frequently found as a surname than as
   a first name.

Melville   From a French placename, meaning
   'industrious one's town'. Variants are Melvyn and
   Melvin.

Melvin   Possibly from the Irish Gaelic, meaning
   'polished chief' or the Old English for 'sword friend',
   or an adaptation of Melville. Also Malvin, Mel,
   Melvyn, Melwin, Melwyn, Melwynn and Vinnie.

Merlin   From Middle English, meaning 'falcon who
   flies low'. The wizard Merlin was an adviser to King
   Arthur. Related names are Marlin, Marlon, Merle,
   Merlinn, Merlyn and Merlynn.

Merrick   The anglicised form of a Welsh variant of
   Maurice.

Merton   From the Old English placename, meaning
   'town by the lake'.

Mervin   From the Old Welsh name Myrddin, meaning
   Merlin, or a variant of Marvin.

Michael   From the Hebrew, meaning 'who is like the
   Lord?', borne in the Bible by the archangel who
   defeats the dragon. Its diminutives and English
   variants are Mick, Mike, Mitch, Micky and Mitchell.
   The Bulgarian form is Mihail; the Czechoslovakian
   Michal, Minka and Misa; the Finnish Mikko; the
   French Michau and Mikhail; the Greek Makis,
   Michail and Mikhalis; the Hebrew Micah; the
   Italian Michele; the Norwegian Mikkel; the Polish
   Michak and Michalek; the Portuguese Miguel; the
   Russian Misha; the Spanish Miguel, Migui and
   Mique; the Swedish Mikael and Mihalje; and the
   Yiddish Michael.

Michel   The French form of Michael.

Mick   A diminutive form of Michael, also used as a
name in its own right.

Mike   A diminutive of Michael.

Mickey, Micky   Diminutives of Michael, also used as
independent names.

Miles   From the Latin *miles*, meaning 'soldier'. A
variant spelling is Myles.

Milo   The German variant of Miles, possibly meaning
'merciful'.

Milton   From an Old English surname and placename,
meaning 'mill town' or 'middle settlement'.

Mitchell   A Middle English variant of Michael. A
surname that became a first name. Variations and
short forms include Mitch and Mitchel.

Mohammed   From the Arabic, meaning 'highly
praised'. The name of the prophet and founder of
Islam. The variants are Mohamad, Mohamed,
Mohammad and Mahomet.

Montague   From an aristocratic surname derived from
a French placename, meaning 'sharply pointed
mount'. Also spelt Montagu. Its diminutives are
Monte and Monty.

Montgomery   From a surname derived from a French
placename, 'mount of a rich man'. A surname that
is sometimes used as a first name, for example, the
actor Montgomery Clift.

Monty   Diminutive of Montague and Montgomery,
also used as an independent name.

Moray   See Murray.

Mordecai   From the Hebrew, possibly meaning
'follower or worshipper of Marduk' (a Babylonian
god). Variants and short forms are Mordechao,
Mordy and Mort.

Morgan   A Welsh name, meaning 'great' and 'bright'.

Morgan le Fay was King Arthur's sister in Arthurian
legend. Sometimes used as a feminine name.

Morris The anglicised form of Maurice.

Mortimer From an Old French placename, Mortemer,
meaning 'dead sea', a stagnant lake. Diminutives
are Mort and Morty.

Morton From the Old English, indicating a 'moor
town'.

Moses A Biblical name of Hebrew or Egyptian origin,
possibly meaning 'saviour' or 'taken from the water'.
Moses led the Israelites out of Egypt and received the
Ten Commandments from the top of Mount Sinai.
The English variants are Moe, Mose, Moshe and
Moss; the French and Italian form is Moise; the
Portuguese Moises; the Russian Moisey and Mosya;
and the Yiddish Moises, Moshe and Mozes.

Muhammad See Mohammed.

Muir From a Scottish surname meaning 'moor'.

Mungo From a Gaelic word meaning 'beloved'.

Murphy From the Irish Gaelic, meaning 'sea fighter'.

Murray Derived from a Scottish Gaelic surname and
placename meaning 'sea'. Also spelt Moray.

Myles See Miles.

Myron From the Greek, meaning 'perfumed oil',
borne by a Greek sculptor of the fifth century. Also
Miron and Myreon.

N

Najib From the Arabic, meaning 'noble parentage'.
Also Najeeb.

Napoleon Of uncertain origin, possibly influenced by

the Italian word for 'lion', *leone*. Napoleon Bonaparte was a nineteenth-century French emperor.

Nat A diminutive of Nathan or Nathaniel.

Nathan From the Hebrew, meaning 'gift', a name borne by a prophet in the Bible.

Nathanael See Nathaniel.

Nathaniel From the Hebrew, meaning 'gift of God'. The variant Nathanael was borne in St John's gospel by an apostle of Jesus, generally identified with Bartholomew. Nathaniel Hawthorne is the American author of the *Scarlet Letter*. Short forms of the name include Nat, Nate, Nathan, Natt and Natty; the French form is Nathanael, and the Italian is Nataniele.

Neal, Neall, Nealle See Neil.

Ned A diminutive of Edmund or Edward. Also Neddy.

Neil From the Irish *niadh*, meaning 'champion'. The name started life as Niall and went back to Britain as Neil. Among the other English variants are Neal, Neill, Neils, Nial, Niels and Niles; the Finnish form is Nilo; the Russian Nil and Nilya; the Scandinavian Niels and Nils; and the Scottish Niall.

Nelson 'Son of Neil', an English surname used also as a first name; for instance, Nelson Mandela.

Neville, Nevil From the French placename Neuville, meaning 'new town'. The Nevilles played a major role in the Wars of the Roses. Its diminutive is Nev.

Newell From the Old English placename meaning 'new hall'.

Newland From the Old English, meaning 'new land'.

Newman From the Old English, meaning 'newcomer'.

Newton From an Old English surname and placename, meaning 'new settlement'.

Nguyen   A Vietnamese family name after a dynasty of
   rulers.
Niall   The original, Irish form of Neil.
Nicholas   From the Greek name Nikolaos, a
   compound of *nike*, meaning 'victory', and *laos*
   'people'. St Nicholas was the patron saint of
   children, and, through the Dutch form of the name,
   is the original Santa Claus. Colette, Nicola, Nicole
   and Nichola are feminine forms. Among its short
   forms are Claus, Cole, Nic, Nick, Nicky and Nik; its
   Bulgarian forms are Nikita and Nikolas; the Dutch
   Nicolaas; the Estonian Nikolai; the French Colin,
   Nicolas and Nicole; the German Claus, Klaus and
   Nikolaus; the Greek Nikolaos, Nikolos and Nikos;
   the Italian Niccolo and Nicola; the Norwegian
   Nicolai; the Portuguese Nicolau; the Russian Kolya
   and Nikolai; the Spanish Nicolas; and the Swedish
   Niklas and Nils.
Nick   A diminutive form of Nicholas.
Nicky   A diminutive form of Nicholas, Nicola and any
   other name beginning with 'Nic', sometimes used as
   a name in its own right. Nikki is a variant spelling.
Nicol   A variant of Nicholas.
Niels   The Danish variant of Neil.
Nigel   From Nigellus, the latinised form of Neil.
Nikita   The Russian form of Anicetus or a diminutive
   of Nicholas.
Ninian   Of uncertain origin, possibly related to
   Nennius, an early Welsh historian, or to Vivian. St
   Ninian was a bishop and missionary. Sir Ninian
   Stephen was a former Governor-General of
   Australia.
Noah   From the Hebrew, meaning 'long-lived' or
   'repose'. The most famous bearer of the name built
   an ark and survived the Flood.

Noel From the French Noël, derived from the Latin *natalis*, meaning Christmas, and usually given to a child born then. Feminine forms are Noele, Noeleen, Noeline and Noelle. Noël Coward is an English actor and playwright.

Nolan From an Irish surname meaning 'famous' or 'noble'. Feminine form is Nola.

Norman From an Old English or Old German name meaning 'man from the north'. The Normans of France were originally from Scandinavia, but the name was already in use in England before the Norman Conquest. Short forms include Norm, Normand and Normie. The feminine form is Norma.

Norton From the Old English surname and placename, meaning 'northern settlement', also used as a first name.

Nowell See Noël.

O

Oakes From the Old English, meaning 'beside the grove of oak trees'.

Oakley An Old English name, meaning 'oak clearing'.

Obadiah From the Hebrew, meaning 'servant or worshipper of the lord'. Borne by the prophet.

Oberon Old German, meaning 'bear-like' and 'noble'. Also Auberon.

Octavius From the Latin, meaning 'eighth', and formerly given by parents of large families to their eighth child. Its variants include Octavio (Spanish), Octavo and Ottavio.

Odo A form of Otto, from the Old German name

meaning 'wealth'. The root of such names as Oates, Oddie and Oates. The feminine forms include Odette and Odile.

Ogden From an Old English surname and placename, meaning 'oak valley'. Ogden Nash was an American humorist.

Olaf From the Old Norse name Anleifr, meaning 'ancestor' and 'relics'. Variants are Aulay, Olav, Olave and Oliver.

Oliver Presumed to be from the Latin *oliva*, meaning 'olive tree'. Oliver Twist is the hero of Charles Dickens's novel of the same name. The French variant Olivier is also used in the English. The Spanish use Oliviero or Oliveros, and the Portuguese form is Olivero.

Ollie A diminutive of Olive and Oliver, or any name beginning with 'Ol'.

Omar From the Arabic, meaning 'supreme follower'. Omar Khayyam was an eleventh-century poet.

Onfroi The French form of Humphrey.

Orlando The Italian form of Roland.

Ormond An Old English placename, meaning 'mountain of bears' or 'spear or ship protector'. Also Ormand and Ormonde.

Orson From the Latin, meaning 'bearlike courage'. In an Old French story, a child named Orson is carried off, and reared in the forest, by a bear. Orson Welles was an actor and director, best known for *Citizen Kane*.

Orville From the French, meaning 'village of gold'. Orville Wright was, with his brother Wilbur, an aviation pioneer.

Osborn, Osborne From the Old English name Ocbeorn, a compound of *os*, meaning 'god' and *beorn*, 'man'. In Old Norse it means 'divine bear'.

The name used to be a surname. Its short forms and variants are Ozzie, Osburne and Osbourne.

Oscar   Derived from the Old English name Osgar, meaning 'sacred sword'. Variants include Oskar and Osker. Oscar Wilde was an Irish poet and dramatist. The statuette awarded annually by the Academy of Motion Picture Arts and Sciences is also called Oscar.

Osmond   From the Old English name Osmund, meaning 'divine protection'. St Osmond was the eleventh-century bishop of Salisbury. Also Osmund.

Ossie, Ossy   Diminutives of Oscar, Oswald or names beginning with 'Os'.

Oswald   From the Old English, meaning 'divine power'. The name was also borne by two saints.

Otis   Old English, meaning 'son of Otto', a variant of Odo. See Otto.

Otto   From the Old German, meaning 'prosperous one'. A name borne by four Holy Roman emperors of the tenth and thirteenth centuries. The French variant is Odon; the Italian Othello; the Norwegian Odo; the Spanish Otilio and Tilo.

Owain   Welsh form of Eugene. See Owen.

Owen   The Welsh variant of Eugene or Ewan, meaning 'well born'.

Ozzie, Ozzy   See Ossie.

P

Pablo   The Spanish form of Paul. Pablo Picasso was an artist.

Paddy   A diminutive of Patrick, also a nickname for

Irishmen. Also Padraic, Paddie, Padraig (rare).

Paolo   The Italian form of Paul.

Paris   From the Old English name 'from Paris', the city. Paris was Helen of Troy's lover.

Parker   From the Old English occupational surname, meaning 'park keeper'. Parke, Parkes and Parks are variants.

Parry   From the Old Welsh, meaning 'Harry's son'.

Pascal   From the Old French, meaning 'Easter child', ultimately from the Hebrew word for 'Passover'. Pascoe is a variant and the feminine form is Pascale.

Pat   Short form of Patrick or Patricia.

Patrick   From the Latin *patricius*, meaning 'noble'. St Patrick was the patron saint of Ireland, who converted the inhabitants to Christianity. Its variants include Padraig, and diminutives Paddy and Pat. The French form is Patrice; the German Patricius; the Irish Padraic; the Italian Patrizio; the Polish Patek; and the Portuguese Patricio.

Paul   From the Latin *paulus*, meaning 'small'. The apostle St Paul was known as Saul until he converted to Christianity, and the name is subsequently borne by many other saints. Among its variants are Pablo, Paulo, Pawel, Pav, Pavel, Pol and Pasha. Its feminine forms are Paula, Paulette and Pauline.

Paxton   From the Old English place meaning 'peace town'. Used as both a surname and first name. Variants include Packston, Paxon and Paxten.

Pearce   See Pierce.

Pearson   See Pierce.

Pedro   The Spanish form of Peter.

Penn   From the Old English, meaning 'pen' or 'enclosure'.

Perce   A diminutive of Percival or Percy.

Percival, Perceval   From the Old French, meaning 'pierce the vale'. The name of one of King Arthur's knights. Parsifal is the German variant and the title of one of Wagner's operas; others include Parsafal, Percey, Purcell and Percivall. The diminutive is Perce.

Percy   From the French, meaning 'hailing from Percy', a village near St Lo. Percy Bysshe Shelley was a poet. Other variants include Pearcy, Percey and Percie.

Peregrine   From the Latin *peregrinus*, meaning 'foreigner' or 'stranger', more generally interpreted as 'traveller' or 'pilgrim'. Its diminutive is Perry.

Perry   A form of Peter or a short form of Peregrine.

Peter   From the Greek *petros*, meaning 'stone', or *petra*, 'rock', a translation of the Aramaic name Cephas. St Peter was the leader of Christ's apostles and the first bishop of Rome. The French form is Piers, which gave rise to such surnames as Pierce and Pearson. In Ireland it was Peader and Pedr in Welsh. The English short form is Pete, and its feminine forms include Peta, Petra and Petrina. Among its many variants are: Petr and Piotr (Bulgarian); Pietr (Dutch); Pierre, and Pierrot (French); Panos, Petros and Takis (Greek); Pedro, Piero and Petro (Italian); Piotr (Polish); Pedro (Spanish); and Petrus (Swedish).

Phelan   From the Celtic, meaning 'wolf'.

Phil   A diminutive of Philip, Philippa or any name beginning with 'Phil'.

Philip, Phillip   From the Greek, meaning 'fond of horses'. Philip was one of Jesus's apostles, and father of Alexander the Great. Its diminutives are Phil and Pip. Philippa, Philipa and Phillippa are the feminine forms. Among the variants are Philippe (French); Philipp (German); Filippo (Italian); Filip and Filya (Russian); Felipe and Felipino (Spanish); and Fischel (Yiddish).

Phineas From the Hebrew, meaning 'oracle', 'mouth of prophecy'. Also spelt Phinehas.

Pierce From the Old Anglo-French, meaning 'rock'. Its variants are Pearce, Piers, Pearson and Pierson.

Pierre The modern French form of Peter.

Piers A French form of Peter.

Pip A diminutive of Philip, also the name of Charles Dickens' hero in *Great Expectations*.

Piran The name of a Cornish saint, also the patron saint of miners.

Placido The Spanish form of Placidius, meaning 'placid' or 'calm'. Placido Domingo is an opera singer.

Porter From the Latin for 'one who guards the door'. A surname sometimes used as a first name.

Prentice From the Old French, meaning 'apprentice'. The spelling variants are Prentis and Prentiss.

Prescott From the Old English, meaning 'from the priest's cottage'. Short forms are Scott, Scottie and Scotty.

Preston From the Old English, meaning 'priest's settlement'. A placename that is used as a surname and as either a first or second name.

Prince From the Latin 'prince'. Variants are Prinz and Prinze.

Q

Qayyim   Arabic for 'right and generous'.

Quentin   Latin for 'fifth'. Variants and diminutives include Quent, Quenten, Quenton, Quint, Quinton and Quintin.

Quigley   Of disputed origins, possibly 'distaff' or 'one with messy hair'.

Quincey   A placename that became a surname and is sometimes used as a first name. Also spelt Quincy.

Quinlan   Irish for 'fit and strong'.

Quinn   Meaning unknown, but a common Irish last name, sometimes used as a first name.

Quinton   A form of Quentin.

R

Rab, Rabbie   The Scottish short form of Robert.

Radcliff   From an Old English surname and placename, meaning 'red cliff'. Also Radcliffe.

Radford   From an Old English placename, meaning 'red ford' or 'ford with reeds'.

Rafael   A variant of Raphael.

Rafferty   From the Irish, meaning 'rich and prosperous'.

Rahim   From the Arabic, meaning 'compassionate'.

Raimondo   The Italian form of Raymond.

Rainer, Rainier   See Raynor.

Ralph   From the Old English Raedwulf, meaning 'wolf counsel'. Variants are Rafe, Raoul, Raul and Rolph.

Ralston   From the Old English placename, 'Ralph's settlement'.

Ramon   The Spanish form of Raymond.

Ramsay, Ramsey   From the Old English surname and placename, meaning 'ram island'.

Ranald   The Scottish form of Reginald. See the related names Reginald, Reynold and Ronald.

Randall   From the Old English name Randwulf, meaning 'shield' and 'wolf'. Randal is a very old variant. Randolph is a variant and the diminutive is Randy.

Randolph   From Randulfus, a latinised form of Randal. Short forms are Rand, Randal, Randall, Randy.

Randy   A diminutive of Miranda, Randall and Randolph.

Raoul   The French form of Ralph.

Raphael, Rafael   From the Hebrew, meaning 'god has healed'. The name borne by the archangel with the power of healing. The Italian painter Raphael was a Renaissance artist. Feminine forms are Raphaela and Rafaela. The diminutives are Raf and Rafe.

Raul   The Roman form of Ralph.

Ravi   From the Hindi, meaning 'conferring'.

Ray   A diminutive of Raymond, often used as a name in its own right.

Raymond   From the Old German name meaning 'counsel' and 'protection', introduced into Britain by the Normans. Ray Lawler is the Australian dramatist who wrote the *Summer of the Seventeenth Doll*. Its German form is Raimund; Italian Raimondo; Portuguese Raimundo; and Spanish Raimundo, Ramon and Mundo. Ray is a diminutive.

Raynor, Rayner   From an Old German name derived from *ragan*, meaning 'might', and *harja* 'army'. Rainer, Rainier, Ranier and Ranieri are other

variants. The feminine forms are Raina and Raine.
Rainer Maria Rilke was a German poet.

Redmond The Irish form of Raymond. Also Redmund.

Reece A form of Rhys, spelt phonetically. Also Rees.

Reeve From the Middle English, meaning 'bailiff'.
Variants are Reave and Reeves.

Reg A diminutive of Reginald. Also Reggie.

Regan From the Irish, meaning 'descendant of a
king'. Variants are Reagan, Reagen and Regen.

Reginald From the Old English name Regenweald, a
compound of *regen* 'counsel' or 'might' and *weald*
'power'. Reynold and Ronald are from the same
root. Its diminutives include Reg, Reggie and Rex.
Among its variants are Rainhold, Reginalt,
Reginauld, Reinald, Reinaldo, Reinhold, Reynold
and Reynolds.

Reilly From the Irish, meaning 'descendant of the
valiant'.

Remy From the French, meaning 'from Rheims', a
central French town that is famous for its brandies
made from champagne.

René A French name, meaning 'reborn', from the
Latin Renatus. The feminine form is Renée.

Reuben From the Hebrew, meaning 'behold, a son'.
A name borne in the Old Testament by Jacob's
eldest son. Variants are Reuban, Reubin, Ruben and
Rubin.

Rex From the Latin *rex*, meaning 'king'. Sometimes
used as a diminutive of Reginald. The variants are
Rey and Reyes.

Reynold A variant of Reginald, meaning 'power and
might'. The French forms are Renauld and Renault;
the Spanish Renaldo, Reinaldo, Rinaldo and
Reynaldo. See also Ronald.

Rhys A Welsh name, possibly meaning 'ardour' or

'rashness'. It has given rise to a number of names, such as Rees, Reece, Rice and Price.

Ricardo   The Spanish and Portuguese form of Richard.

Richard   From the Old German name Ricohard, meaning 'dominant ruler', a name introduced into Britain at the time of the Norman Conquest. Its diminutives include Dick, Dickie, Dicky, Dixon, Rich, Richie, Rick and Ricky. Its German variant is Richart; the Greek Rihardos; the Hungarian and Norwegian Rikard; the Italian Ricardo; the Polish Ryszard; and the Spanish Ricardo and Rico.

Richmond   From the Old German, meaning 'powerful protector'.

Rick, Ricky, Rickie   Diminutives of Derek, Eric and Richard, also used as names in their own right.

Rider   From the Old English, meaning 'horse rider'. Also Ryder.

Riley   From the Irish, meaning 'brave'. Variant spellings are Reilly and Ryley.

Riordan   From the Irish, meaning 'bard, minstrel'. Also spelt Rearden and Reardon.

Ripley   From an Old English placename, meaning 'from the shouter's meadow'.

Roald   A Scandinavian name, derived from the Old German 'known for strength'. Roald Amundsen was a Norwegian explorer.

Rob, Robbie   Diminutives of Robert or Robin, also used as a name in its own right.

Robert   From the Old German name Hrodebert, meaning 'fame' and 'bright'. The name was introduced into Britain during the Norman Conquest. The name was made famous in the fourteenth century by Robert the Bruce, King of Scotland. Its diminutives and variants include Bert, Bob, Bobbi, Bobby, Rob, Robbie, Robby, Robin and

Rupert. The Czechoslovakian form is Rubert; the
French Robin, Robers and Robinet; the German
Rudbert and Ruprecht; the Irish Riobard; the Italian
Roberto, Ruberto and Reperto; and the Spanish
Roberto, Ruperto and Tito.

Roberto   The Italian form of Robert.

Robin   A variant of Robert, and also a bird. Robin
Hood was an outlaw of English folklore. Its
diminutives are Rob and Robbie, and the feminine
form is Robyn.

Robinson   From the Old English, meaning 'son of
Robert'.

Rocco   Italian for 'rest'. Variants are Roch, Rocky,
Roche and Rock.

Rochester   From an Old English placename meaning
'stone camp'. Short forms are Chester, Chet and Rock.

Rock   From the Old English meaning 'from the rock'.
Also a variant of Rocco and Rochester.

Rocky   A variant of Rocco.

Rod, Roddy   Diminutives of Roderick or Rodney, also
used as names in their own right.

Roderick   From the Old German name Hrodric,
meaning 'fame' and 'rule'. Its diminutives are Rod,
Roddie, Roddy, Roderic, Rodrich and Rory. The
German form is Roderich; the Italian Rodrigo and
Roderigo; the Spanish Rodrigo and Ruy.

Rodger   See Roger.

Rodney   From the Old English, meaning 'island close
to the clearing', also a placename. Short forms are
Rod and Roddy.

Rodrigo   The Spanish and Italian form of Roderick.

Roger   Also Rodger. Derived from the Old English or
Old German words for 'fame' and 'spear'. The
French form Roger entered Britain at the time of the
Norman Conquest. Rodge is its diminutive. Its

variants are Rutger, Ruttger, Rudiger and Rogerio.

Rohan   A form of Rowan, and also the Hindi for 'sandalwood'.

Roland   From the Old German, meaning 'famous land'. Rowland is a variant, as is Orlando (in the German, Italian, Spanish). The English variants include Rolland, Rollin, Rollins, Rollo, Rolly and Rowe; the German Rudland and Ruland; the Italian and Spanish Rolando; the Polish Rolek; the Spanish Rolon, Rollon and Roldan.

Rolf   From the Old German, meaning 'swift wolf'. Also Rolph. A related name is Rudolph.

Rollo   A variant of Rolf or a diminutive of Roland.

Rolph   See Rolf.

Romeo   From the Italian, meaning 'pilgrim to Rome'. Shakespeare's play of a pair of star-crossed lovers featured Romeo and Juliet.

Ron   A diminutive of Ronald.

Ronald   The Scottish form of the Old Norse equivalent of Reginald. Diminutives are Ron and Ronnie. Related names are Ranald, Reginald and Reynold.

Ronan   From the Irish, meaning 'little seal'.

Ronnie, Ronny   Diminutives of Ronald, also used as names in their own right.

Rory   From the Gaelic, meaning 'red'. Also used as a short form of Roderick.

Ross   From the Scottish Gaelic, meaning 'promontory'. The feminine form is Rosslyn.

Rowan   Either from the name of a tree or from the Gaelic *ruadh*, meaning 'red'. Variants include Roan, Rowe and Rohan.

Rowland   See Roland.

Roy   From the Gaelic, meaning 'ruler'. Also Roi and Rey.

Ruben See Reuben.

Rudolf See Rudolph.

Rudolph From the Old German, meaning 'famous wolf', related to Rolf. English variants and short forms include Rolfe, Rollo, Rolph and Rudy. The Czechoslovakian form is Ruda, Rudolf and Rudek; the French Rodolphe; the German Rudolf, Rutz; the Hungarian Rudi; the Italian Rudolfo and Rodolfo; the Polish Rudek; the Slavic Rudi; and the Spanish Rodolfo, Rolo, Rudolfo, Rudi, Rudy and Rufo.

Rudy, Rudi Diminutives of Rudolph, also used as independent names.

Rufus From the Latin, meaning 'red'. Variants are Ruffus and Rufous.

Rupert A variant of Robert, based on the modern German form of Hrodebert.

Russ A diminutive of Russell, also used as a name in its own right.

Russell From the Old French *roux*, meaning 'red', originally given to someone with red hair or a ruddy complexion.

Ryan From the Irish Gaelic, meaning 'little king', and a common surname in Ireland.

S

Sacha The Russian diminutive of Alexander, 'defender of humankind'. Also Sascha and Sasha.

Said From the Arabic, meaning 'cheerful'. Also Saeed, Sayeed and Sayid.

Salomon The French and Hungarian form of Solomon.

Salih Arabic for 'righteous one'. Also Saleem.

Salman Muslim name meaning 'high'.

Salvador The Spanish form of Salvatore.

Salvatore An Italian name, derived from the Latin *salvator* 'saviour'. Its variants are Salvador, Xavier, Xaviero and Zavier.

Sam A diminutive of Samson, Samuel or Samantha, sometimes used as a name in its own right.

Sameer Muslim name meaning 'small breeze'.

Samson From the Hebrew, meaning 'sun child'. The Samson of the Old Testament possessed great strength. Its diminutives are Sam and Sammy. Sampson is a related form.

Sammy, Sammie Pet forms of Samuel and Samson.

Samuel From the Old Hebrew, meaning 'name of God' or 'heard by God'. The Old Testament prophet who anointed Saul and David as the first kings of Israel. The Italian forms are Salvatore and Samuele; the Yiddish Shem, Shemuel and Schmuel; the German Zamiel and Hungarian Samie.

Sanders Middle English for 'son of Alexander', or the Greek for 'defender of humankind'. Variants include Sanderson, Saunders and Saunderson.

Sandy A diminutive of Alexander or Sandra, sometimes used as a name in its own right.

Sanjay From the Sanskrit, meaning 'conscience'.

Saul From the Hebrew, meaning 'asked for'. The name was borne in the Old Testament by the first king of Israel.

Sawyer From the Old English, meaning 'woodsman'.

Saxon Derived from the Germanic 'from Saxony', latinised to Saxon; ultimately from a word meaning 'dagger' or 'short sword'.

Scott A name derived from the surname meaning

'Scot' or 'Scottish', probably first used as a nickname in England.

Seamus   The Irish form of James, 'he who supplants'. Also Seamas and Shamus.

Sean   The Irish form of John. (Shaun and Shawn are anglicised spellings.) The original Irish was Eoin.

Searle   From the Old English for 'shield'.

Sebastian   From the Latin Sebastianus, 'of Sebastia', a town in Asia Minor; ultimately derived from the Greek, meaning 'venerable'. St Sebastian was a Christian martyr, usually depicted as a man shot through with arrows (he was subsequently clubbed to death). Its short forms are Bastian and Seb. The French form is Sébastien; the Italian Sebastiano.

Selby   From a surname and a placename meaning 'willow farm'.

Selwyn   A name of disputed origins: from the Old English *sele* 'house' and *wine* 'friend' or from the Latin name Silvanus. Also Selwynn and Selwynne.

Septimus   From the Latin, meaning 'seventh', and formerly given by parents of large families to their seventh child.

Serge   The French form of Sergius.

Sergei   The Russian form of Sergius.

Sergio   The Italian form of Sergius.

Sergius   From the Latin, meaning 'attendant'. St Sergius was a priest who was martyred in Cappadocia in AD 304.

Seth   From the Hebrew, meaning 'compensation, substitute'. Seth was the third son of Adam and Eve, regarded by Eve as a replacement for her dead son Abel.

Seumas   See Hamish, Seamus.

Seward   From the Old English, meaning 'sea victory' and 'guard'.

Sextus From the Latin, meaning 'sixth', and formerly given by parents of large families to their sixth child.

Seymour An aristocratic surname derived from the Old French, 'from St Maur'. St Maur was a Benedictine monk of the sixth century.

Shamus See Seamus.

Shane A variant of Sean, and therefore John.

Shannon From the Irish, meaning 'old river', and the name of the River Shannon in Ireland. The name is used for both boys and girls.

Sharif From the Arabic, meaning 'honest'. Also Shareef.

Shaun See Sean.

Shelby From and Old English name, meaning 'from the ledge estate'. See also Shelley.

Sheldon From an Old English surname and placename, meaning 'steep-sided valley' or 'flat-topped hill'.

Shelley, Shelly From an Old English surname and placename, meaning 'ledge meadow'. Once used for both boys and girls, these days it is almost exclusively a girls' name.

Shem From the Hebrew, meaning 'fame'. The name of Noah's eldest son in the Old Testament.

Sheridan From the Irish, possibly meaning 'wild man'.

Sherwood From the Old English, meaning 'shire'. Sherwood Forest was home to Robin Hood.

Sid A diminutive of Sidney, also used as an independent name.

Sidney, Sydney From 'St Denis', Dionysus. A famous English last name used as a first name in the eighteenth century.

Siegfried A German name, derived from the Old

German *sigu* 'victory' and *frithu* 'peace'. Also spelt Siegfrid and Sigfried.

Sigmund   From the Old German, meaning 'victorious protector'. Sigmund Freud was an Austrian psychoanalyst. Variants include Sigismund and Zygmunt.

Silvanus   From Latin, meaning 'wood dweller'. Variants include Silvain, Silvano, Sylvanus and Sylvio.

Silvester   See Sylvester.

Sim   A diminutive of Simon.

Simeon   From the Hebrew, meaning 'listening', borne in the Old Testament by the second son of Jacob and Leah.

Simon   A variant of Simeon, possibly influenced by the Greek *simos*, meaning 'snub-nosed'. The French form is Simion and Simeon; the German Sim; the Italian Simone; the Rumanian Simion; the Yiddish Shimon. Its feminine forms are Simona and Simone.

Simpson   'Son of Simon'.

Sinclair   From a Scottish surname derived from the French placename St Clair. (Clair means 'bright' and 'clear'.) Related name is Clarence.

Sloan   From the Irish, meaning 'armed warrior'. Sloane is a variant.

Smith   From the Old English occupational surname for 'blacksmith', perhaps more commonly used as a surname than a first name. Variants include Smyth and Smythe.

Solomon   From the Hebrew *shalom*, 'peace'. In the Old Testament, Solomon was the wise king of Israel. The feminine equivalent is Salome.

Somerset   From an Old English placename, meaning 'summer settlement'. Somerset Maugham was a writer. Variants include Sommerset and Summerset.

Spencer   A Middle English occupational surname

meaning 'provisioner'. The name has been associated with the Churchill family since the eighteenth century. Variants are Spence and Spenser.

Stacy A diminutive of Anastasia or Eustace, often used as an independent name, but is now given almost exclusively to girls. Stacey is a variant spelling.

Stafford From an Old English placename, meaning 'landing place ford'. Variants are Stafforde and Staford.

Stamford From the Old English for 'stony ford'. A placename sometimes used as a first or second name.

Stan A diminutive of Stanley. See Stanley.

Stanislas From the Polish name Stanislaw, probably derived from the words meaning 'glorious camp'. The patron saint of Poland, St Stanislaus, was an eleventh-century bishop and martyr.

Stanley From an Old English placename, meaning 'stony field'.

Stanton An Old English name, meaning 'stony place or farm'.

Stefano The Italian form of Stephen.

Stephan The German form of Stephen.

Stephen, Steven From the Greek *stephanos*, meaning 'crown'. St Stephen was the first Christian martyr, and the name was subsequently borne by a number of other saints and popes. The feminine forms are Stefanie, Stephanie and Stevie. The Bulgarian, Czechoslovakian, Polish and Swedish form is Stefan; the French is Etienne and Tiennot; the Greek Stamos, Stefanos and Stavros; the Portuguese Estevao; the Russian is Stenya; and the Spanish is Esteban.

Steve   A diminutive of Stephen, also used as a name in its own right.

Stewart   See Stuart.

Stirling   From the Old English, meaning 'genuine' or 'top quality'. Early English money was called sterling.

Stuart   From a Scottish surname ultimately derived from the Old English *stigweard*, meaning 'steward'. The name has associations with the house of Stuart (or Stewart), the ruling dynasty of Scotland and England. Stewart was the original form of the surname; Stuart was adopted during the reign of Mary, Queen of Scots. Diminutives include Stew and Stu.

Sulaiman, Suleiman   Arabic forms of Solomon.

Sullivan   From the Irish, meaning 'descended from the hawk-eyed'.

Sven   Norwegian, meaning 'youth'. The Danish form is Svend, Swen and Swenson.

Syd   See Sid and Sidney.

Sydney   See Sidney.

Sylvester   From the Latin, meaning 'of (or in) the woods'. The name was borne by a fourth-century pope.

T

Taggart   From the Gaelic, meaning 'son of the priest'.

Tait   From the Old Norse, meaning 'cheerful'. Spelling variants include Tate and Tayte.

Talbot   Of uncertain derivation, but may be from the Middle English, meaning 'wood-worker'.

Talib   An Arabic name, meaning 'seeker of truth'.

Taliesin   A Welsh name, meaning 'radiant brow'. Taliesin was a Welsh bard of the sixth century.

Tam   A Scottish diminutive of Thomas.

Tane   Polynesian for the god of light and nature, the supreme and beneficent god.

Tanner   An occupational surname, meaning 'leather worker'.

Taro   A Japanese name, often given to first-born sons. Loosely translates as 'big boy'.

Taylor   An Old English occupational surname meaning 'tailor' or 'cutter'.

Teague   From the Irish, meaning 'bard, poet'.

Ted   A diminutive of Edmund, Edward or Theodore, a name that dates back to the fourteenth century. Pet forms include Teddy and Teddie.

Templeton   From the Old English, meaning 'village near the temple'. Short forms include Temp and Temple.

Tennessee   A Native American/Cherokee name, now used for the American state. Probably its most famous namesake is the playwright Tennessee Williams (originally christened Thomas).

Tennyson   From the Middle English, meaning 'heir of Dennis'.

Terence, Terrence   Derived from the Roman clan name Terentius. Publius Terentius Afer was a second-century BC dramatist. Terry is the diminutive. The German form is Terenz and the Spanish Terencio.

Terry   A diminutive of Terence. Also a variant of Theodoric, the French form of the name.

Thaddeus   Aramaic for 'praise the Lord' or Greek for 'courageous and stout-hearted'. The name borne by one of Christ's twelve apostles. The English short forms include Tad, Tadd, Taddy and Thaddy; the Czechoslovakian is Tades and Tadaes; the German

Thaddaus; the Italian Taddeo; the Polish Tadzio and the Russian Thaddej.

Theo A diminutive of any name beginning with Theo, sometimes used as a masculine name in its own right.

Theobald Derived from the Old German name Theudobald, meaning 'brave people'. Shakespeare's Tybalt in *Romeo and Juliet* is possibly a variant of Theobald.

Theodore From the Greek, meaning 'God's gift'. The name was borne by several saints and one American president. The short forms are Ted, Teddie, Theo and Tudor; the feminine form is Theodora. Other variants include Fedor and Feodor.

Thom A diminutive of Thomas, which gave rise to the surname Thompson. The variant spelling Tom has been the more common form.

Thomas From the Aramaic, meaning 'twin'. A name borne in the New Testament by one of the twelve apostles. English diminutives are Tam, Tammy, Thom, Tom and Tommy. The feminine forms include Thomasin, Thomasina and Thomasine. Tomas is a popular variant, used throughout Europe.

Thornton Derived from a surname and a placename, ultimately from the Old English, meaning 'thorn wood'.

Tien From the Chinese, meaning 'heaven'.

Timothy From the Greek name Timotheos, meaning 'honoured by god'. In the Old Testament Timothy was Paul's companion. Short forms are Tim and Timmy.

Titus From the Greek, meaning 'of the giants'. Borne in the first century by the Roman emperor Titus Flavius Vespasianus, and by the giant who was slain by Apollo. The Italian form is Tito and the Greek Titos.

Tobias From the Hebrew, meaning 'god is good'. The name occurs in the Old Testament. Its variants include Toby, Tobin and Tobiah.

Toby The anglicised form of Tobias, also a diminutive of the name. Toby is often used as an independent name.

Todd From a surname meaning 'fox'.

Tom A diminutive of Thomas, also used as a name in its own right.

Tomi From the Japanese, meaning 'wealthy'. From the Nigerian, meaning 'the people'.

Tommy A diminutive of Thomas, also used as a name in its own right.

Tony A diminutive of Anthony, also used as a name in its own right.

Toshio Japanese for 'year boy'. The short form is Toshi.

Travis From the Old French, meaning 'crossing or tollgate keeper', an occupational surname that became a first name. Its variants are Traver, Travers and Travus.

Trefor See Trevor.

Tremain A Cornish surname meaning 'place or farm at the stone'. Also Tremayne and Tremaine.

Trent From the Latin, meaning 'flowing stream'.

Trevor From a surname derived from the Welsh name Trefor, meaning 'large village'. Its diminutive is Trev.

Tristam A variant of Tristan.

Tristan From the Celtic name Drystan, meaning 'din', influenced by the French *triste*, 'sad'. The medieval story of Tristan, who falls in love with the Irish princess Isolde, has inspired a number of literary and musical works. Its variant is Tristam.

Troy   From an Irish name, meaning 'foot soldier' or from the French placename Troyes. Troy was the site of the Trojan War.

Truman   From the Old English, meaning 'loyal one'. Truman Capote was an American author and Harry Truman an American President.

Tudor   The Welsh form of Theodore.

Tung   From the Vietnamese, meaning 'stately'.

Turner   An occupational name from the Middle English, meaning 'woodworking master'.

Ty   A diminutive of Tyrone and Tyler.

Tyler   From the Old English occupational name, meaning 'maker of tiles'.

Tyrell   From the name of a Roman clan. Also Tyrrell and Terrell.

Tyrone   From the name of an Irish county, ultimately from the Gaelic, meaning 'Owen's land'.

Tyson   From the Old French, meaning 'firebrand'.

U

Uberto   Spanish and Italian forms of Hubert.

Ulric   Appears in Old English as Wulfric, meaning 'wolf' and 'power'.

Ulysses   The Latin form of Odysseus. French forms are Ulisse or Ulysse.

Ulrik   German, Slavonic and Danish form of Ulric.

Umberto   The Italian form of Humbert, also the name of the last king of Italy.

Upton   Old English for 'upper place or farm'.

Urban   Latin for 'from the city'. Eight popes bore the

name Urban. Its variants are Urbain, Urbaine, Urbano and Urbanus.

Ure   A diminutive of Uriah or Uriel.

Uriah   Hebrew for 'light of Jehovah'.

Uriel   An angel name meaning 'light' and 'radiance'.

V

Vaclav   Czechoslovakian for 'wreath of glory'. See also Stephen.

Valentine   From the Latin *valens*, meaning 'strong' or 'healthy'. Valentina is the feminine version, and the pet form Val is shared with Valerie. The Italian form is Valentino, others include Valencio and Valentyn.

Van   Dutch for 'son of', originally a nickname. Van is also a feathered monster or dragon in Armenian myth.

Vance   Middle English for 'thresher'.

Vassily   Russian form of Basil or William.

Vaughan   A Welsh first name and surname, Vaughan is the anglicised form of *fychan*, a Welsh word meaning 'little'.

Vernon   A French placename from the Gaulish word 'where alders grow'. Also Vern and Verne.

Victor   Meaning, the winner. The Welsh form is Gwythyr. Short forms are Vic and Vick. The Hungarian form is Viktor; the Italian Vittorio; the Portuguese is Vitor; the Russian is Vika, the Vitenka and Vitya; and the Spanish forms are Victorio, Vito and Victorino.

Vincent   Comes from the Latin verb *vincens*, 'to

conquer'. Short forms are Vince, Vinnie, Vinny
and Vin. The French form is Vincenz; the
Italian is Vincenzo or Enzo; and the Spanish is
Vincente.

Virgil Latin for 'flourishing' or 'staff bearer'. Also the
name of the Roman epic poet (70–19 BC), author of
the *Aeneid*.

Vito From the Latin meaning 'of life'. Also a Spanish
form of Victor.

Vladimir Old Slavic for 'powerful warrior' or 'army
ruler', the Russian form of Walter.

Vyvyan Also spelt Vyvian, and originally a masculine
name, with Vivien and Vivienne the feminines.
From the Latin Vivianus, meaning *vivus*, 'alive'.
This distinction is now blurred. Viv is the diminutive
of all these.

Wade Old English for 'from the river crossing'.

Wagner From the German, meaning 'wagonmaker'.

Walcott Old English for 'cottage near the
embankment'. Short form is Waldo.

Walden An Old English name, meaning 'child of the
forest valley'. Also spelt Waldon.

Waldo From a German word meaning 'power', also a
short form of Waldemar or Valdemar, which means
'great ruler'.

Walker Old English for someone who walked on
cloth to clean it.

Wallace Originally Saxon for 'foreign', *waelisc*, to be
from Wales. Another form is Wallis, used for boys

and girls. The short forms Wal and Wally are shared
with Walter.

Walt   A short form of Walter. Also used in its own
right.

Walter   From the Old German meaning 'rule-people'.
Wally and Walt are short forms. French forms
include Gautier and Gauther; the Russian Vladimir,
Volya and Vovka, and Bualterio; Gualterio and
Gutierre in the Spanish.

Wandjuk   Aboriginal name.

Wang   Chinese for 'regal'.

Ward   Old English for 'guardian' or 'watchman'.

Warner   Old German for 'the defending army' or
'defending warrior'. German forms include Werner
and Wernher.

Warren   The German *Varin* means to 'watch, guard'.

Warwick   A placename used as a surname and first
name, the Old English meaning is 'buildings close
to the weir'. Warrie is used as a short form.

Wata   Maori form of Walter.

Wayne   From *wain*, the old word for a cart or wagon,
and would have been a name given to a cartmaker.

Wellington   Old English for 'town by the welling
stream'. The name of many places, including the
capital of New Zealand.

Wendell   Old German for 'seeker'.

Wentworth   Old English for 'a hut occupied in winter'.
A common surname given as a second name.

Wenzel   Slavonic name meaning 'to know'. See also
Stephen.

Werner   German form of Warner.

Wesley   Old English for 'field in the west'. Also spelt
Wesly, Wessley, Westleigh and Westley.

Whitney   From the Old English, meaning 'from the
white island; from fair water'. Short form is Whit.

Wilbur   From the Old German *wil* and *burh*, meaning 'will' and 'defence'.

Wilfred   A combination of Anglo-Saxon *will* and *frith*, 'will' and 'peace'. Short form is Wilf.

Will   Short form of William.

Willem   Dutch form of William.

William   From the Old German words *vilja* ('will') and *helma* ('helmet'). Will, Bill, Billy are the most used English diminutives. The Irish form is Liam, the French Guilliame and Guillot. Feminine form is Wilhelmina.

Willie, Willy   Short forms of William.

Willis   A form of William.

Wilson   'Son of Will', also a variant of William.

Wilton   Old English meaning 'from the farm with a spring'. Short forms include Will, Willie and Willy.

Wim   Dutch and German diminutive of Wimpje (William).

Winston   A placename made up of Old English elements meaning 'joy' and 'stone'. Winnie is a short form, other variants are Wynstan, Wynston and Winsten.

Wolfgang   From the Old German for 'advancing wolf'. Wolfgang Amadeus Mozart was an Austrian composer.

Woodrow   Old English for 'row of bushes or trees near the woods'.

Woody   Short form of names containing the prefix wood. Also a name in its own right: Woody Allen and Woody Harrelson.

Wright   'Carpenter' or 'joiner' in the Old English; an occupational surname.

Wyatt   From the French, meaning 'little warrior'.

Wyndham   Old English for 'hamlet near the wandering path'.

Wynn Welsh for 'fair one', also spelt Win, Winn and Wynne.

Wynton From a Welsh word, meaning 'white place'.

Wystan A form of Winston, Teutonic for 'wise' and 'stone'.

X

Xavier Arabic for 'bright, brilliant'. St Francis Xavier is the patron saint of missionaries. The English form is Javier; the German Xaver; and the Italian Xaviero.

Xenos Greek for 'a guest' or 'a stranger'.

Xerxes Persian for 'ruler'. Xerxes was the king of Persia in the fifth century BC.

Ximen, Ximenes Spanish forms of Simon.

Y

Yaakov Hebrew form of Jacob.

Yael Hebrew for 'mountain goat'. Also a girls' name.

Yahya Arabic form of John.

Yale Old English 'from the slope' or 'fertile moor'.

Yasir Arabic for 'wealth'. Also spelt Yaseer and Yasser.

Yehudi Hebrew for 'praise the Lord' or 'Jewish'. A variant of Judah.

Yevgeny The Russian form of Eugene.

Yitzhak The Israeli form of Isaac.

Yorick A form of George.

York Old Celtic for 'from the yew estate', or Old

English for 'from the estate of the boar'. Also spelt Yorke.

Yü Chinese for 'jade'.

Yule Old English for 'born on Christmas'. Yul is a variant.

Yusha Arabic form of Joshua.

Yusuf, Yussef Arabic forms of Joseph.

Yves The French form of Ives, 'little archer' or 'son of the yew bow'. Variants include Eouan and Euzen.

Z

Zach Short form of Zachariah, also an independent name.

Zachariah Hebrew for 'Jehovah has remembered'. English variants are Zach, Zack and Zak; the French is Zacharie; the German is Zacharia; the Russian is Zakhar, Swedish and Norwegian are Zakris.

Zacharias Hungarian variant of Zachariah.

Zafar Muslim name meaning 'accomplishment'.

Zander A form of Sander, the diminutive of Alexander.

Zane An English form of John, 'gracious gift of God'.

Zeeman Dutch for 'seaman', a common name for those born under the water signs.

Zelman A form of Solomon.

Zia Muslim name for boys and girls meaning 'enlightened'.

Zubin Hebrew for 'exalt'. Zubin Mehta is a famous conductor.

Zygfryd The Polish form of Siegfried.

Zygmunt The Polish form of Sigmund.

GIRLS

A

Abby, Abbey, Abbie Short forms of Abigail.

Abigail A Hebrew name meaning 'a father's joy', found in the First Book of Samuel. It appeared in Britain in the sixteenth century and was very popular until it became a slang term for a 'lady's maid'. Short forms include Abbey, Abbie, Abby, Gael, Gail, Gaile, Gael, Gale and Gayle, all now used as independent names. A Hebrew variant is Avigayil.

Ada Teutonic for 'noble'; Hebrew for 'adorned beautifully'.

Adelaide A name with a long European history, closely associated with 'Ethel' and 'Alice'. It comes from the Old German *athal*, meaning 'noble' or 'highborn'. The capital of South Australia was named in 1836 after Queen Adelaide, who brought popularity to the name in Britain. Associated forms include Adela, Adele, Adelinde, Adeline, Alina and Alyna.

Adena, Adina, Adinah A Hebrew name, meaning either 'gentle, delicate' or 'adorned, ornamented'. Short forms are Dena and Dina.

Adina Aboriginal for 'good'; Hebrew for 'noble'; Greek for 'delicate'.

Adriana Italian feminine form of Adrian, from the Latin Hadrianus, meaning 'of the Adriatic' (Sea). The name probably came from the Latin for 'black', the port of Adria having dark sand. Associated forms include the French Adrienne, Adrianne, and Adriane.

Adrienne From the Latin, meaning 'dark, rich'. Variants include Adriana, Adriane and Adrianna.

Affrica   A very old Irish and Manx name from the Celtic name Aifric, meaning 'pleasant'. Also Affrika, Affrikah. This derivation is not related to the name of the continent, whose origins are unclear.

Agnes   From the Greek, meaning 'pure, chaste'. St Agnes was a Roman maiden martyred in the third century. The Spanish form is Inez.

Aida   Arabic for 'reward, present'. Italian form of Ada, and the title of a popular opera by Verdi.

Aileen   See Eileen.

Aimée   The French form of Amy.

Aine   An Irish name meaning 'delight, rapture', it was once a boys' name but is now used mainly for girls. Aine was the Irish goddess of love and fertility.

Aisha, Aiysha, Ayesha   A popular Arabic name meaning 'life, alive', borne by the favourite wife of the Prophet Mohammed. Used in many Muslim countries including Egypt, Turkey and Islamic Africa, and also in non-Muslim countries, with minor spelling variations. Other forms are Ayasha, Ayeisha, Ayisha and Asha.

Aisling, Aislinn   An Irish name which means 'a dream or vision'.

Alabama   After a southern state of America.

Alana, Allana, Alannah   Possibly from the Irish for 'Oh my child', it is used as a term of endearment in Ireland. Some believe it to be a feminine form of Alan. Variants include Alanis, Alanna, Alannah, Alina, Allana. Shortened forms are Lana, Lane and Lann.

Alberta   Female form of Albert; from the Old German for 'noble' or 'bright'. Also the name of a province in Canada. Variants and diminutives include Albertina, Albertine, Elberta, Elbertine, Bert and Berta, the Greek Alverta, and Czechoslovakian Alba.

Aleema, Alema, Alima Muslim name meaning 'scholarly, literary'.

Alessandra An Italian form of Alexandra.

Alexandra A feminine form of the Greek name 'Alexander', which means 'protector or defender of humankind'. A name associated with Russian and British royalty. Its variants and pet forms include Alexandria, Alexandrina, Alex, Alexa, Alexia, Alexis, Sandra and Zandra. The French forms include Alexandrine, Alexandrie and Alix; the Italian Alessandra and Alessandrina; the Bulgarian Alekko and Sander; the Czechoslovakian Leska and Lexa; the Russian Sasha and Sashenka; the Spanish Alejandra and Jandina; the Greek Aleka and Ritsa.

Alexis From the Greek for 'protector' or 'defender'. It was originally used as a Russian name for boys, but it became popular in other countries, including America and England, in the early 1900s and is now used for both sexes.

Ali A pet form of Alice, Alison, Alicia, and other 'Al' names.

Alice Has a complex history and is associated with Adelaide and Ethel, derived from Adalheidis, the Old German name meaning 'nobility'. *Alice's Adventures in Wonderland* (1865) by Lewis Carroll helped to popularise the name. Its variants include Alesia, Alicia, Alisa, Alisha, Alyse, Alysa, Alysia, Alyissa. The Polish form is Alicja; the Welsh is Alys. Pet forms include Ali, Allie and Ally.

Alicia English variant of Alice.

Alida From the Greek city in Asia Minor where people were 'beautifully dressed' or the Latin for 'small and winged'. Also Aleda, Alidia and Lida.

Alina Another name from *athal*, the Old German for

'noble', related to Adeline. Also Aline, Aleen,
Alena, Alene.

Alison Originally a diminutive of Alice but has
become a name in its own right. Also Allison,
Alisoun, Allyson. Diminutives include Ali, Allie,
Ally, Lissi, Lissie and Lissy.

Alix Diminutive of Alexandra.

Allegra Italian for 'lively, joyful and merry', after the
musical term *allegro*.

Althea A Greek name, from the Latin for 'healer' or
'wholesome', from *althaia*, the marshmallow plant
with healing properties.

Alys The Welsh form of Alice.

Alyssa A Greek name meaning 'rational', it comes
from the flowering plant alyssum. Similar to some
alternative forms and spellings of Alice.

Amalia An alternative form of Amelia, from the
Gothic word for 'hard-working'. Used in various
European countries including Germany, Poland,
Rumania and Hungary.

Amanda Meaning 'worthy to be loved' or 'lovable', it
is part of a group of names that come from the Latin
amare, to love. Amanda was possibly a
seventeenth-century literary invention. Short forms
include Mandy and Mandie.

Amara A Greek name meaning 'eternally beautiful',
or the name for paradise in the legends of Abyssinia
(now Ethiopia).

Amber From the Arabic *anbar*, for ambergris. One of
the 'jewel' names which became popular in the
nineteenth century. Amber is a rich yellow fossil
resin used to make jewellery. A Muslim variant of
the name is Ambreen.

Amelia Probably comes from the Gothic word for
'hard-working'. Related to Emily. Variants include

Amalia, Amalie, Amela, Ameline, Amelinda and
Amelita. Short forms are Milly and Millie, which are
also used in their own right.

Amina, Aminah, Ameena   Muslim name meaning
'honest, dependable'. Amina was Muhammed's
mother.

Amira, Ameera   A Muslim name meaning 'princess'.

Amy   From the French Aimée, meaning 'beloved'.
Also Amie and Ami. Variants include the Spanish
Amada and Amata.

Anastasia   Greek name meaning 'rising again' or
'resurrection'. In the past given to babies born at
Easter time. Pet form Stacey is also a name in its
own right.

Andrea   A feminine form of Andrew, from the Greek
for 'manly'. Variants include Andee, Andra,
Andreanna, Andrée, Andriana, Andrina and
Andrietta. Pet forms include Andy, Andie, Dreena,
Drina and Rena.

Angel   From the Greek for 'messenger'. The many
forms include Angela, the French Angèle and the
Italian diminutive Angelina.

Angela   A feminine of the Greek *angelos* for angel
('messenger'). English and European variants
include Angelica, Andela, Angelika, Anjela,
Angeliki, Angyalka, Angelique and Angeline.
Shortened forms are Anje and Angie.

Anisa, Aneesa   Muslim name meaning 'tender, loving'.

Anita   The Spanish form of Ann, used independently.
The pet form is Nita.

Ann, Anne   A very old English name from the Hebrew
for 'grace' or 'favour', a variant of Hannah. The
mother of the Virgin Mary, according to apocryphal
gospels, was called Anna. Princess Anne of
Luxembourg helped spread the popularity of the

name from Russia and Bohemia to England in the fourteenth century as wife of Richard II. From the seventeenth to the nineteenth century it was one of the most used English names. British variations include Anne, Anna, Hannah and Nancy with pet forms Annie and Nan. The many European forms and variants include the French Annette and Nanette; the Spanish Ana and Anita; the Italian Anna, Annica and Ninetta; the Danish Annika; the Czechoslovakian Anicka, Andula and Anuska; the German Anneliese, Annali and Hanne; the Polish Anka; the Finnish Annikki; the Estonian Anya (also Russian and Latvian) and Anyula; the Latvian Annushka and Asenka; the Russian Anninka. Compounds include Anne Marie, Annel and Marianna.

Anna   A variant of Hannah. It was the Latinised form of Anne and become popular in the English-speaking world in the nineteenth century.

Annabel, Annabelle   Variants of Amabel, a popular name in the Middle Ages derived from the Latin for 'lovable', which was itself superseded by its pet form Mabel. Annabella is a variant; Belle a diminutive.

Anneliese   A German formation of Anna and Liesa (Elisabeth). Also Annalisa, Annelisa and Annelise.

Anona, Nona   Welsh. A variant of 'Non', after a fifth to sixth-century saint, or from the Latin for ninth.

Antoinette   See Antonia.

Antonia   Feminine forms of Anton or Anthony (from the Latin for 'priceless'). Antonetta is a Swedish form; Antonina Russian; Antonieta Spanish; and Antoinette French. Diminutive is Toni, Tonia or Tonya.

Anya   A variant of Anne used in Russia, Latvia and Estonia.

April   After the fourth month of the year.

Arddun   Welsh name meaning 'beautiful'.

Aretha   From the Greek for 'virtuous'. Also Arete, Arette, Oretta.

Ariadne   'Holy one' or 'divine one'. According to Greek myth, Ariadne assisted Theseus to navigate the Minotaur's labyrinth with a golden thread. Italian forms are Ariana and Arianna; the French form is Ariane.

Ariana, Arianna   Italian forms of Ariadne.

Ariane   The French form of Ariadne.

Ariannell   A Welsh girls' name. Ariannell was an early Welsh saint.

Ariel   From the Hebrew, meaning 'lioness of God'. Variants include Arielle and Ariella. Milton and Shakespeare had male 'Ariels' but the name is now usually given to girls.

Artemis, Artemisia   Greek goddess of hunting, chastity, and protector of children and youth. Diana was her Roman equivalent.

Ashleigh, Ashley   From the Old English for 'from the meadow of ash trees', originally a surname that came to be used as a first name. Sometimes spelt Ashlea, Ashlee and Ashlie. Also a boys' name.

Asia   After the continent.

Aster   From the Greek for 'star'. One of a number of star names, it is also the name of a daisy. Also Asta, Astera, Astra.

Astrid   A Scandinavian name, meaning 'divine power' or 'divine beauty'.

Athena, Athene   The Greek warrior goddess of wisdom, after whom the Greek capital Athens was named.

Atalanta, Atlanta   According to Greek legend, Atalanta was a beautiful huntress, who would only marry a man who could out-run her. Atlanta is the capital city of Georgia, USA.

Aubrey   From the Old French form of the Old German for 'elf counsel', brought to England form Normandy.

Audrey, Audree   A form of Etheldreda found in the 1500s, which became an independent name. Variants include Audra, Audree and Audry.

Aurora   The Roman goddess of the dawn who sheds golden light, the name comes from the Latin *aurum*, meaning 'gold'. The French variant is Aurore.

Autumn   After the season.

Ava   Probably a variant of Eva, from the European pronunciation of the name.

Aviva   From the Hebrew 'springtime' or 'springlike', symbolic of youth. A variant is Avivi.

Awena   Female form of Welsh name meaning 'muse', from the Old Breton *anaw*, meaning 'wealth'.

B

Baba   Swiss pet form of Barbara.

Babette   A variant of Elizabeth and Barbara; originally a French diminutive for the names.

Bailey   From the Old French 'bailiff'. A surname now used as a first name for boys and girls.

Bano   Muslim name meaning 'woman'.

Barakah, Baraka   Arabic name which means 'blessings'.

Barbara   Greek name meaning 'a stranger' or 'foreigner' (from the same root as 'barbarian'). St Barbara was a third-century martyr who is said to be the patron of architects and engineers, and a protector against thunder and lightning. Variants include Barbra, Barbara-Ann; the Russian Varvara; the Czechoslovakian Barbora; and the Spanish Barbarita. Diminutives include Babs, Barb, and Barbie, in Scotland Baubie, in France Barbe, in Poland Basia and Germany Barbchen.

Basha   Variant of Batya.

Basia   Polish pet form for Barbara and also Hebrew variant of Batya.

Basma   Swahili name meaning 'smile'.

Batya, Batyah   Hebrew name meaning 'daughter of God'. Found in contemporary Israel. Also Basia, Basya, Basha.

Bea, Bee   Short forms of Beatrice.

Beatrice, Beatrix   From the Latin, meaning 'one who brings joy'. Short forms Beata, Beatta, Bea, Beatty, Beattie and Trixie. Russian forms Beatrix, Beatrisa, Spanish form Beatriz, Scots form Beitris.

Becky, Beck   Diminutives of Rebecca.

Bedelia   See Bridget, although the diminutive Delia is often used in its own right.

Belinda   Old German, probably from *lindi*, meaning 'serpent', and 'sacred' or 'wise'. Diminutives include Linda, Lindy, Bindi and Belle.

Bella   A short form of Isabella and Anabella, or from the Italian for 'beautiful'.

Belle   French for 'beautiful'.

Benedicta   Feminine form of Benedict, from the Latin Benedictus, meaning 'blessed'.

Benita   Spanish diminutive of Benedicta.

Berenice   Girl's name from the Greek meaning 'bringing conquest'. Alternative form in Greece is Berenike. Related to Bernice.

Bernice   Variant of Berenice.

Bernadette A French feminine form of Bernard (from the Anglo-Saxon for 'bear-hard'). Pet form Bernie, also used as a name in its own right.

Bernadine, Bernadina Feminine forms of Bernard.

Bernie Diminutive of Bernadette, Bernadine, Berenice, Bernice and the masculine Bernard, or a name in its own right.

Berry After the small fruit.

Bertha From the Old German, meaning 'shining'.

Beth Diminutive of Elizabeth or Bethany.

Bethany A placename from the New Testament, the home of Lazarus. Variant is Bethanie.

Bettina Originally a diminutive of Benedicta, found now as a name in its own right.

Betty, Betsy Traditionally popular diminutives of Elizabeth. Betty was often used in the sixties in America as a compound, for instance, Betty-Sue. A variant is Bette.

Beulah A Hebrew name which means 'married'.

Beverley A placename and surname which came from the Old English for 'beaver stream' in Yorkshire, England. Also a surname, it was once used for boys but this is now rare.

Bevin A Scottish surname, used as a personal name for boys and girls.

Bian Vietnamese name, meaning 'hidden, secretive'.

Bianca, Biancha From the feminine form of the Italian word *bianco*, meaning 'white'.

Biata A Polish name for girls.

Bibi An Arabic name meaning 'a king's daughter'. Also a pet form of Bibiana.

Bibiana, Bibbiana From the Latin for 'lively'. The pet form Bibi can be used independently.

Bijou French for 'jewel'.

Billie Originally from the pet form for William, now

used independently and for girls.

Bindi Short form of Belinda.

Bindu A Sanskrit Hindu name for girls which can mean 'pearl' or 'the truth'.

Binny, Binnie Pet form of Bianca or Benedicta.

Birgitta, Birgit, Brit See Bridget.

Blair This Scottish name (meaning 'a plain') has journeyed from placename to surname, to boys' name and now girls' name.

Blaise, Blaze, Blase From the Latin for 'stutterer'. Used for boys and now girls.

Blanche The French feminine for 'white'. Blanche d'Alpuget is an Australian novelist.

Blanka A Czechoslovakian, Danish, German and Norwegian form of Blanche.

Blinne, Blinnie An Irish girls' name.

Bliss Anglo-Saxon name later favoured by Puritans, it means 'state of joy'.

Blodwen, Blodwyn A Welsh name meaning 'white flower'.

Bobbi, Bobbie, Bobby Diminutives of Roberta.

Bonita This Spanish name is a variant of Bona, from the Latin for 'good'.

Brandy, Brandi From the name of the drink.

Brenda From the Old English, meaning 'firebrand'. A feminine form of Brandon and Brendon.

Briana, Brianna, Breanna, Bryanna A Gaelic name, this is the feminine of Brian, meaning 'strength' or 'hill'. Variants Brianne and Brienne. Diminutives Bree, Brie.

Bridie Irish diminutive of Bridget.

Bridget, Bridgit, Brigid An old Irish name which may mean 'strength' or 'high one'. The name of an Irish goddess and later an abbess who became a saint. Other Irish forms include Brigit and Brighid, with pet forms Bridie and Biddy; French forms include Brigitte and Brigette; the Polish Brygida and Brygitka; the Italian Brigidina and Brigida; and the Scandinavian Birgitta and Brigitta with pet forms Brit and Birgit.

Briony, Bryony Disagreement as to origins; may be from the Latin for a vine or climbing plant.

Brittany Placename from the Latin for 'from Britain'. Brittany is a province in France.

Brontë Possibly after the surname, in honour of sisters and writers Charlotte, Emily and Anne.

Bronwen, Bronwyn A Welsh name meaning 'white breasted'.

Bronya A variant of Bronwen.

Brooke From the Old English surname meaning 'dweller by the brook'.

Bryn, Brynn Welsh name for girls.

Bryony See Briony.

Buchi A Nigerian name. Buchi Emecheta is a successful Nigerian female writer.

C

Caddie After the Sydney barmaid who thought her life would make a good story and wrote her autobiography, made into a film starring Helen Morse. Caddie was short for a 'Cadillac', to which she was compared as a compliment. Caddie can also be an abbreviation of Caroline.

Cai Vietnamese name for girls, meaning 'female'.

Caitlin, Kaitlin, Caitlyn, Kaitlyn, Catelyn, Katelyn, Catlyn A form of Catherine ('pure'). Kathleen is the anglicised version. Among the short forms are Cate and Kate.

Caledonia From the Latin for 'from Scotland' and a placename – Caledonia Canal is in Scotland and New Caledonia is a group of islands in the Pacific whose capital is Nouméa.

Calliope A Greek name, after the muse of epic poetry. The Greek form is Kalliopi; the pet form, Popi.

Calypso Another figure from Greek mythology, a sea nymph who kept Odysseus on her island of Ogygia for seven years. Also refers to the name of an impromptu ballad style from the West Indies.

Camilla First used in the early thirteenth century in Britain. It was an Etruscan name for the young helpers of the priests at religious ceremonies. Camilla was the name of a swift-footed virgin Queen of an Etruscan tribe immortalised by Virgil in the *Aeneid*. Camille is a French variant; the Czechoslovakian form is Kamila; the Polish Kamilla. Pet forms include Cam, Cammie and Millie or Milly.

Camille The French form of Camilla, meaning 'young ceremonial attendant'.

Candace, Candice From the Greek for 'glowing white'. This was a hereditary name or title of Ethiopian queens. Pet forms Candi, Candida, Candy and Kandy.

Caoimhe An Irish name meaning 'charm' or 'beauty', and the name of an Irish saint.

Caprice An Italian name meaning 'subject to whim, impulsive', as in 'capricious'.

Cara, Kara From the Italian *caro* or the Latin *carus* for 'dear, beloved'. Variants Carina, Carine, Karina.

Carina, Karina, Carine Variants of Cara.

Carla A feminine form of Carl or Charles.

Carlotta An Italian form of Charlotte. The Spanish form is Carlota, the short form Lola.

Carly, Carley, Carlie A feminine form of Carl or Charles, or a diminutive of Carla, Carlotta or Caroline. See Charles.

Carmel From the Hebrew for 'the garden', after Mt Carmel in Israel, where a convent and church were dedicated to the Virgin Mary. Variants are Carmela, Carmelita, Carmelina and Carmina.

Carmen This name is the Spanish form of Carmel, although it is sometimes said to be connected to the Latin word for 'song' or 'poem'.

Carol One of the feminine forms of Charles, this was originally a diminutive of Caroline which is also used as an independent name. Variants include Carole, Carolle, Karol.

Carolina Italian and Spanish form of Caroline, and also after the American state. Other forms include the Ukrainian Russian and Polish Karolina.

Caroline Another feminine form of Charles or Carl via the Latin form Carlo. The name was popularised in the eighteenth century in England, and has been used in Australia since the arrival of the First Fleet. Carolyn was a later development of the name used in the last fifty years. Diminutives are Carrie, Carry and Caro. Variants include Carolyn, Carolin, Carolynne and Carolina.

Carolyn Variant of Caroline.

Carrie, Carry, Carey, Cari, Carri, Kari Usually familiar forms of Carol, Caroline, Carolina and variants. Sometimes used independently.

Carys A Welsh name meaning 'love'.

Casey Of unclear origins. It may be Irish Gaelic for 'watchful' or a diminutive of Acacia, or another name such as Cassandra or the Polish Casimir. Can

112

be a surname and a boys' name as well as a girls'
name. Many spelling variants, including Casee,
Caisi, Casie, Kaysey, Kaysee and KC.

Cassandra   According to Greek myth the beautiful
Cassandra was given the gift of prophecy by
Apollo, but when she rejected him he decreed that
no-one would believe her warnings. Short forms are
Cass and Cassie.

Cass, Cassie   Diminutives of Cassandra, sometimes
used independently.

Cassia   A Greek name referring to a cinnamon-like
spice. See also Kezia.

Cassidy, Kassidy   An Irish surname meaning 'clever',
which has come to be used as a personal name for
boys and girls.

Catalina   Spanish form of Catherine.

Cate, Kate   Short form of Catherine and Katherine.

Caterina   Italian form of Catherine.

Catherine, Katherine, Catharine, Katharine,
Kathryn   The Greek word *katharos* means 'clean' or
'pure', and this has come to be the accepted
meaning of the word. The first recorded Catherine
was a virgin martyr. Short forms include Cath, Kath,
Cathy, Kathy, Cate, Kate, Catie, Katie, Katy and
Kitty. Some of the many forms include the Polish
Katatzyna, Kassia, Kaska and Kasienka; the Spanish
Catalina and Catana; the Italian Caterina; the
Russian Katya, Katinka, Katerinaka, Katka and Kisa;
the Welsh Catrin; and the Irish Cathlin, Caitrin and
Caitlin.

Cathy, Kathy   Common diminutives of Catherine or
Kathleen, or independent names.

Cathleen, Kathleen   From the Irish Caitlin.

Catrin   A Welsh form of Catherine.

Catriona, Caitriona, Catrina, Katrina   An Irish name

derived from the Old French form 'Caterine'
(Catherine). Triona is a diminutive.

Cécile French form of Cecilia.

Cecilia A feminine form of Cecil, derived from the
Latin *caecus*, meaning 'blind', this was a popular
name in the Middle Ages. The Roman St Cecilia, a
singer, was a patron of musicians and music, and in
177 died as a martyr. Its variants include Cecile,
Cecilie, Cecily and Celia. The Irish form of Celia,
'Sile', gave rise to Sheila and Sheelagh.

Cecily, Cecilie Two of the many variants of Cecilia.

Celeste, Celestia From the Latin for 'heavenly' or
'divine', the original form is the French Céléste,
which is a boys' name. Variants include the French
Celestine, Celie and Céléste; the Spanish Celestina
Chela and Chila; the Polish Celestyna, Cela,
Celinka and Celina; the Czechoslovakian Celestyna,
Tyna and Tynka.

Celia Variant of Cecilia.

Celine, Celena From the French name Céline,
probably from the Latin *caelum*, meaning 'sky' or
'heaven'. Possibly related to Celia or Celeste.

Celinka A Polish form of Celeste.

Cera, Ceara Irish name for girls which may mean
'bright red'.

Chambeli A Hindi name meaning 'jasmine'.

Chamji A girls' name from the Himalayas.

Chandler From the French for 'candle maker'.
An occupational surname used as a personal
name.

Chantal, Chantelle From a French placename
meaning 'stony place'. It is perhaps related to the
French verb *chanter*, 'to sing'.

Charis A Greek name which means 'grace'. Variants
are Charissa and Charisse.

Charissa, Charisse   Variants of Charis.

Charity   From the Latin *charitas* for Christian love. One of the 'abstract quality' or virtue names favoured by the English Puritans in the 1600s. One of the three daughters of St Sophia, the other two being Faith and Hope.

Charlene   A familiar form of Caroline and Charlotte.

Charlotte   A feminine form of Charles, derived from the Italian Carlotta. Pet forms are Charlie, Lotty and Totty. The French form is Lolotte, the Italian Carlotta, Spanish and Portuguese Carlota, and the Greek Karlotta.

Charmaine   Of uncertain derivation, possibly a form of Carmel, Carmen or Charmian.

Charmian   Derived from a Greek word meaning 'a little joy'. Shakespeare used the name for one of Cleopatra's slaves in *Antony and Cleopatra*. Charmian Clift was an Australian writer.

Charo   A Spanish pet name for Rosa ('rose').

Chelsea   An English placename, from the Old English for 'port' or 'harbour'. Chelsea is a London suburb.

Cherie   From the French *chérie*, 'darling'. Also Sherry and Sherri.

Cherry   Originally a diminutive of Charity. Sometimes used as a name in its own right, and also as a variant of the French Cherie.

Cheryl, Sheryl   A name of disputed origins, but possibly a variant of Cherry, which was popular mid-century.

Chiara   Italian form of Clare, meaning 'clear, bright'.

China   A Shona name from Zimbabwe for girls born on Thursday. Also after the country of that name.

Chiquita   Spanish name meaning 'little one'.

Chloe   A Greek name meaning 'a new green shoot'.

One of the names of Demeter, the Greek goddess of agriculture.

Chris Diminutive of names for boys or girls beginning with 'Chris' including Christine, Christina and Christopher.

Christel German form of Christina. See also Crystal.

Christina, Christine Derived from the Old English for 'Christian'. One St Christina was a Roman martyred in the third century. Christine was derived from the French form of Christina. Christina Stead was an Australian writer who wrote *The Man who Loved Children*. Short forms include Chris, Chrissy, Chrissie, Christy, Christie, Kris, Krissy, Kristy, Tina, Teena. Variants include Kristine, Kristina, Christen, Kristen, Kirsten; the Polish forms Krystyna and Krysta; the French Crestienne; the German Christiane, Christel and Christa; the Italian Cristina and Christiania; the Russian Khristina and Tina; the Czechoslovakian Krystina and Krista; and the Greek Kristos.

Chrystal, Crystal, Krystal See Crystal.

Ciara, Ciar An Irish name meaning 'black, dark'.

Cilla Diminutive of Priscilla.

Cindy A diminutive of *Cinderella*, which has come to be used as a name in its own right, or a pet form of Cynthia or Lucinda.

Clarissa From the Latin, meaning 'most brilliant'. A modern form of Clara.

Clare, Claire, Clair Clare comes from the Latin for 'bright, clear' and also 'renowned'. In the thirteenth century St Clare of Assisi founded the convent of nuns known as 'Poor Clares'. The Latin form 'Clara' was in vogue in the nineteenth century and Klara is found in a number of European countries. Claire is the French form of the name.

Clarissa   From the Latin, meaning 'most brilliant'.
A modern form of Clara.

Claudia   Feminine version of 'Claud', from the Latin
for 'lame'. Found particularly in France. French
variants include Claudine and Claudette.

Claudine, Claudette   French variants of Claudia.

Clelia, Clelya   Italian name for girls, derived from the
Latin for 'glorious'.

Clementine   From the Latin *clemens*, merciful. Also
Clementina. Masculine form is Clement.

Cleo, Clio, Klio   Diminutives of Cleopatra.

Cleopatra, Kleopatra   Greek name from Kleopatra,
meaning 'her father's fame'. The name of a number
of Egyptian female royals, most famous of whom
was Queen Cleopatra who had liaisons with both
Julius Caesar and Mark Antony.

Clodagh   An Irish name, after an Irish river.

Cody, Codie   From the Old English for 'pillow' or
'cushion'. Used for both boys and girls.

Colette   Derived from a diminutive of Nicolette,
which became a name in its own right. Name of the
French writer whose works included the *Claudine*
series.

Colleen   An Irish word meaning 'girl', which is
actually not often used as a personal name in
Ireland. Colleen McCullough wrote the bestseller
The Thorn Birds.

Connie   A short form of Constance.

Constance   From the Latin, meaning 'firmness'.
Constanza and Constantine are variants.

Cora   From the Greek word *kora* meaning 'girl'.
Variants are Corinna, Coretta and Corinne.

Coral   A substance produced by small sea animals out
of which jewellery is made. Jewellery names
became fashionable in the nineteenth century.

Cordelia   Of unknown etymology, used by
Shakespeare for King Lear's youngest daughter.
The pet form is Delia.

Corey, Cory   Used for both sexes, it may be an Irish
name meaning 'from the hollow'. May also be a
familiar form of Cora.

Corrina   Possibly a diminutive of Cora, from the
Greek for 'girl'. See also Carina.

Corinne   The French form of Corrina.

Cosima   An Italian name, feminine of Cosmo, which
means 'order'.

Courtney, Courtenay   A noble surname from the Old
English for 'from the court' or the Old French for
'short nose'. The name has been used for both sexes
as a personal name.

Cristina   Italian form of Christine, Christina.

Crystal, Chrystal, Cristal, Krystal, Krystle   From the
Greek for 'ice', 'frost'. Associated with jewel and
gem names that were fashionable in the late
nineteenth century.

Cybil   From the Latin, a form of Sybil. Also spelt
Cybill.

Cyndi   Alternative form of Cindy.

Cynthia   In Greek myth Cynthia was a name given to
the goddess Artemis, referring to the fact that she
was born on Mt Cynthus on Delos in the Aegean.

Czarna   A Slavic name popular in Jewish families that
means 'black', referring to a woman with dark eyes
or dark hair.

D

Dacey From the Irish Gaelic meaning 'from the
south, southerner'. Also Dacie, Dacy.

Dae An English name meaning 'day'.

Dairine Irish name for girls, which may be the
feminine of Daire, meaning 'productive'.

Daisy, Daisie A flower name, from the Old English for
'day's eye'. It started to be used as a girls' name in
the nineteenth century, initially as a translation of
the French girls' name Marguerite.

Dakota From the Native American Sioux nation, this
word means 'friend'. Also the name of the American
state.

Dale, Dayle From an Old English placename which
means 'valley'. Also used as a boys' name.

Dallas An Irish name meaning 'wise, skilled', and the
name of another American city.

Damaris A Greek name meaning 'gentle', relating to
'a calf'.

Dana An Irish goddess of fertility and abundance
(also called Danu and Ana), or Celtic for 'from
Denmark'. The name is also given to boys.

Danica, Danika A Slavonic name meaning 'morning
star', or from a Danish word meaning 'a Dane'.

Danielle A French feminine form of Daniel (from the
Hebrew for 'God has judged'). Variants Daniella
and Danita. See also Daniel.

Danu See Dana.

Daphne From the Greek, meaning 'laurel tree'.

Darcy, D'arcy, D'Arcie From the Irish for 'dark', or
an English placename and surname after a
place in France called Arcy. Also a boys'
name.

Daron An Irish name used as a feminine form of Darren.

Dasha A Russian diminutive of Dorothy (from Greek for 'gift of God').

Davida, Davita Feminine forms of David (from the Hebrew for 'beloved'). Davida Allen is an Australian artist. Also Davina.

Dawn From the Old English, meaning 'first light of morning'.

Debbie Short form of Deborah.

Deborah, Debra, Debrah A Hebrew name meaning 'a bee'. The biblical Deborah was a prophetess who called the Israelites to rebel against the Canaanites. The name was taken up by the Puritans in the seventeenth century and became very popular. It arrived in Australia with the First Fleet. Other forms include Devorah, Devora and Devra.

Dee Short form of any name beginning with 'D', or an independent name.

Deirdre An Irish name which may mean 'broken-hearted', 'chatterer' or 'raging'. According to Irish and Scottish folklore, the beautiful Deirdre killed her lover and then herself. Also Derdriu, Deidre.

Delaney Irish surname sometimes used as a personal name.

Delia A Greek name after the island Delos, birthplace of Apollo and Artemis, and another name for Artemis. Also a diminutive of Bedelia and Cordelia.

Demeter After the Greek goddess of agriculture and fertility, and mother of Persephone. Variants include Demetria and Demetris.

Demi A Greek short form of Demeter, or French for 'half'.

Denise From the Greek, meaning 'a follower of

Dionysus', the Greek god of wine and intoxicating herbs who was raised by nymphs in India. The French feminine form of Dennis.

Dennie, Denny   Pet forms of Denise, sometimes used independently.

Désirée   From the French, meaning 'longed for'.

Deva, Devi   Hindu Sanskrit name meaning 'divine, godlike'. A name for the goddess of the moon.

Devon   From the Old English, a county in the English south.

Devorah   A variant of Deborah ('a bee').

Devra   Diminutive of Devorah.

Diana, Diane, Dianne   Diana was the Roman goddess of fertility, hunting and the moon, the twin sister of Apollo.

Dianthe   A Greek name meaning 'flower of the Gods'.

Dione, Dionne   Feminine forms of Dennis.

Dita   Short form of Perdita, from the Latin for 'lost'.

Dixie   From the Latin (and French) for 'ten'.

Djamila   See Jamilla.

Dobah   A Hebrew name meaning 'a female bear'.

Dolores   From the Spanish, meaning 'sorrows'. See also Lolita.

Dominica   From the Latin, meaning 'of the Lord'. Also Dominique.

Donna   From the Latin, meaning 'lady'.

Dora   From the Greek, meaning 'gift'. See also Dorothy.

Dorotea   A Spanish and Italian form of Dorothy.

Dorothy   A Greek name from *doron* and *theou*, meaning 'Gift of God'. Dorothy was the most popular girls' name during World War One. The variant Dorothea was fashionable in the 1800s. Short forms Dot and Dotty. Variants include the German Dorothea and Dorlisa; the French Dorothée

and Dorette; the Spanish and Italian Dorotea; the
Polish Dorota and Dorosia; and the Russian Dorofei,
Daschenka and Dorka.

Drozha   Slavic Jewish name meaning 'my little dear
one'.

Drusilla   From the Roman clan name, Drusus. Also
Druscilla, Drucilla.

E

Eartha   From the Old English for 'the earth'. Eartha
Kitt is an African-American singer.

Ebony, Ebonie   Meaning 'black', from the tropical
trees that have black hard wood.

Ebrilla   A Welsh name which means 'April'.

Eda   From the Old English for 'rich and happy'.

Edana   A Celtic name meaning 'fiery', the feminine of
Aidan. St Edana was an Irish saint after whom a
holy well with healing properties was dedicated.

Eden   From the Hebrew for 'enjoyment, pleasure'.
The biblical reference is 'Paradise', the garden
where Adam and Eve lived. Eden has been used as
a first name for both sexes.

Edie   A short form of Edith, also used as an
independent name.

Edith   From the Old English for 'prosperous war'.
The name was used widely in Anglo-Saxon times
in the form Eadgyth, till the Normans arrived. Its
form gradually changed to Edith. The pet form is
Edie.

Edna   From the Hebrew for 'rejuvenation'.

Edwina   From the Old English *ead*, compounded with

'wine', meaning 'happy wealthy friend'. A modern feminine form of Edwin.

Effie   From the Greek, meaning 'pleasant speech'. A short form of Euphemia.

Eileen   From the Irish 'Eibhlin', which may be a form of Helen or may be derived from Evelyn or Evelina. Also Aileen, Ayleen.

Eimer, Emer   An Irish name for girls. According to Irish folklore Eimer was the wife of Cuchulainn.

Eira   A Welsh name for girls meaning 'the snow'.

Eirawen   A Welsh name for girls meaning 'snowy white'.

Eirian   A Welsh unisex name meaning 'silver'. Variants include Eirianedd and Eirianell.

Eithne   An Irish name which may be derived from the Irish for 'nut-kernel', 'fire' or 'gorse'. Eithne was the mother of the Irish sun god. See also Enya.

Ekaterina   Slavic variant of Katherine.

Elain   A Welsh name for girls meaning 'fawn'.

Elaine   Derived from 'Helaine', an Old French form of Helen ('the bright one'). Used as a personal name from the mid-nineteenth century.

Elan   From the Welsh for 'to drive or push', and the name of several Welsh rivers.

Eleanor, Eleanora   A name of uncertain etymology, which went to England from France in the twelfth century. The derivation was believed for many years to be from the Greek 'Helen', which may be the case, although Latin derivations have been proposed. Variants include Elinor, the Italian forms Eleonora and Leonora, and French Eleonore and Lenore. The diminutive is Nora.

Elen   A Welsh variant of Helen.

Eleni   Greek form of Helen.

Elisabetta   An Italian form of Elizabeth.

Elise A French form of Elizabeth (or Eliza).

Elissa An alternative name for Dido, the legendary Queen of Cathage, who killed herself when she was abandoned by Aeneas. May be a form of Alice or Elizabeth.

Eliza A short form of Elizabeth used as a name in its own right since the eighteenth century, and one of the most popular names in England in the nineteenth century. Variants include the Czechoslovakian form Eliska and the Italian, Latvian and French Elisa.

Elizabeth, Elisabeth Derived from the Hebrew, meaning 'God has sworn' or 'God is satisfaction'. A classic English name, greatly favoured by royalty. Many diminutives exist, including Bess, Bessie, Beth, Betsy, Bettina, Betty, Elisa, Eliza, Libby, Libbie, Lis, Lisabet, Liz, Liza, Lizette, Lizzie. Other forms and diminutives include the German Elisabet, Elsbeth and Elschen; the Hungarian Liszka, Sziszi, Zizi, Zsizsi and Zsoka; the Italian Elisabetta, Bettina and Lisettina; the Lithuainian Elzbieta and Elzbiyeta; the Czechoslovakian Alzbeta, Beta, Betka, Betuska and Eliska; the Polish Elzbietka, Elzunia, Ela and Elka; and the Russian Elisavetta, Lisenka, Elisabete, Yelizaveta, Betkhen and Lizka.

Ela Polish form of Elizabeth.

Ella from the Old English, meaning 'friend of the elves'. Ella Fitzgerald was a renowned American jazz singer.

Elle See Ellen.

Ellen An early English form of Helen. Diminutives are Elle, Elly, Ellie, Nelly and Nellie.

Ellie, Elly Diminutives of Eleanor, Ella and Ellen.

Eloise The French form of Louise. Also Heloise.

Elsa From the Old German, meaning 'noble'. Also a familiar form of Elizabeth. Variants include Else, Elsie, Ilsa and Ilse.

Emily An English name derived from the Roman clan name Aemilius. Short forms are Milly and Millie. Variants include the Bulgarian, Rumanian, Polish, Italian and Spanish Emilia; the Czechoslovakian Emilie; the Latvian Emiliya; and the Spanish Emiliana.

Emma Derived from *ermin*, the Old German name for 'universal' or 'all embracing'. Pet forms Em and Emmie. Variants Emmeline and Emmelina.

Emmeline A variant of Emma.

Enid A Welsh name meaning 'spirit, soul'.

Enya Anglicised form of Eithne.

Erica Feminine form of Eric, 'ever-powerful'.

Erin, Erynn An Irish Gaelic name from *eireann*, meaning 'western island', a very old name for Ireland. Variants are Erinne, Eryn, Erynn and Erynne.

Esperanza A Spanish name meaning 'hope'.

Eudora From the Greek meaning 'happy gift'. Dora can be a short form.

Eugenia, Eugénie From the Greek for 'nobility'. Found in England in the twelfth century. Eugenie is the French form, borne by the wife of Napoleon III, the Empress Eugenie (1826–1920).

Eulalia From the Greek for 'sweetly speaking'. St Eulalia was the patron saint of Barcelona, where she was martyred. Variant Eulalie.

Eunice From the Greek for 'good or happy victory'.

Euphemia See Effie.

Eva, Eve From the Hebrew meaning 'lively' or 'life-giving'. According to the bible the name of the first woman, Adam's partner. Short forms Ev, Evvie. Evita is a variant.

Evadne   A Greek name of uncertain etymology.

Evalina   Possibly from the Old German name Avelina, or the Old French *aveline*, meaning 'hazelnut'.

Evelyn   From a surname derived from Aveline. Used also as a boys' name. Variants are Eileen, Eveleen, Evelina and Eveline.

Evita   See Eva.

Evonne   Variant spelling of Yvonne, popularised by Australian tennis player Evonne Goolagong (Cawley).

F

Fabiana   After the name of a Roman clan, possibly derived from the Latin meaning 'bean' or 'bean-grower'. Fabian is the masculine form and the French form is Fabienne.

Fabienne   French form of Fabiana.

Fairley, Fairlie, Fairlee   Possibly from the Old English for 'a beautiful meadow'.

Faith   One of the abstract virtue names favoured by the Puritans, this began to be used as a first name after the Reformation. Faith was one of the three daughters of St Sophia in early Christian times, the other two being Hope and Charity. Variants Faythe and Fayth. Fay was possibly derived from Faith.

Fallon   From the Irish Gaelic, meaning 'descendant in a ruling family.'

Fanya   Russian form of Frances.

Faren, Farren, Faron   A name of uncertain etymology, possibly from a surname.

Farrah   From the Middle English for 'attractive, pleasant'. Also Farra, Farah.

Fatima, Fatimah   Favoured daughter of the Prophet Mohammad, who married Ali. This popular Arabic name is favoured throughout the Islamic world. Also Fatma.

Fay, Faye   First found in England at the end of the nineteenth century, it may be a variant of 'Faith' or may be from *fay*, meaning 'fairy'.

Fee   Short form of Felicity or Phoebe.

Felicia   See Felicity.

Felicity   From the Latin *felicitas* for 'lucky' or 'happiness', and the feminine form of Felix. Alternative forms are Felicia and Felice, with short form Fee.

Fenella   This is the English form of the Gaelic Fionnghuala or Fionnuala, meaning 'white shouldered'. Finola is the Irish form.

Fern, Ferne   After the plants.

Fernley   From the Old English for 'fern lea' or 'fern meadow'. A placename used sometimes as a personal name.

Ffion, Fionn, Finn, Fin   An Irish Gaelic name for both sexes which means 'fair-headed'.

Fifi   A French short form of Josephine.

Filippa   Variant of Phillipa.

Finola   Variant of Fenella, with short form Nola.

Fiona, Ffiona   Taken from the Gaelic *fionn*, meaning 'white, fair', which is a prefix to many Irish names. This name was apparently coined by William Sharp, a nineteenth-century Scots writer, to create his pseudonym 'Fiona MacLeod'.

Flann   An Irish name for boys or girls meaning 'brightest red', 'red as blood'.

Fleur   The French word for 'flower'.

Flora From the Latin *flos*, meaning 'flower', after the Roman goddess of flowers, springtime and youth, whose festival was called 'Floralia'. Found in many countries, with Italian form Fiore, French form Flore, and Russian forms Flora, Lora, Lorka.

Florence From the Latin for 'blooming, flourishing'. Diminutives include Flo, Floss and Flossie. Variants include the Spanish Florida; the Italian Fiorenza; and the French Florette.

Florida Spanish variant of Florence. The southern American state was so named because of its floral splendour.

Fontaine After the French for 'fountain'. Also spelt Fontane, Fontayne.

Forest, Forrest A surname used sometimes as a personal name.

Fotina Greek form of Frances.

Fran Diminutive of Frances.

Franca Diminutive of the Italian Francesca or Francisca.

Frances Feminine form of the Latin Franciscus, which although literally meaning a 'free person', came to mean a person of French origin. The name has many European variants, and first appeared in Italy and France in the thirteenth century, and in England in the fifteenth century. The male form Francis was also used for females until the seventeenth century. Diminutives include Frankie, Franci, Francie, Fanny, Franny and Fran. French forms are Françoise and Francette; the Spanish Francisca; the Greek Fotina; the Italian Francesca; the German Franziska; the Hungarian Franci and Ferike; and the Romanian Francise.

Francesca Italian form of Frances.

Franci   Hungarian form of Frances.

Francine   A French pet form of Françoise.

Françoise   French form of Frances.

Frankie   Diminutive of Frances (or Frank) or a name in its own right.

Franny   Diminutive of Frances.

Frederica, Frederique   The feminine form of Frederick, from the Old German for 'peace ruler'.

Freya   From Freyja, the Norse goddess of love, fertility and beauty.

Frieda   A feminine form of Frederick, of German origin. Freda is a spelling variant. See Frederick.

Fuyuko   Japanese name meaning 'winter'.

G

Gabby, Gabbie, Gabi   Diminutives of Gabrielle.

Gabrielle   A feminine form of Gabriel (Hebrew for 'man of God'), of French origin.

Gabriella   Italian feminine form of Gabriel.

Gaenor   A more traditional Welsh spelling of Gaynor.

Gaia, Gaea   In Greek mythology, the goddess of earth who was the daughter of Chaos. She was the mother of Uranus, the heavens, and Pontus, the sea. The Romans identified her with the earth goddess Tellus. Also known as Ge, Gea.

Gail, Gale, Gayle, Gayl   Probably from the short form for Abigail, which became an independent name.

Garnet   Middle English, a surname possibly meaning 'safety, protection', that came to be used as a boys' name. The trend to jewel names at the end of the last century influenced its use as a girls' name. A garnet is a deep-red gem.

Gay From the Old French *gai*, meaning 'cheerful, merry'.

Gaynor The more commonly seen phonetic spelling of the Welsh Gaenor, which itself came from Gwenhwyvar or Guinever.

Geena See Gena.

Gemma Probably derived as the feminine form of James. Also 'gemstone' in Italian. Alternative spelling Jemma.

Gena Originally a short form of Eugenia, now used in its own right. Also Geena and Gina.

Geneva Possibly from the Old French for 'juniper berry', related to Jennifer. The name of the city and the lake in Switzerland.

Genevieve A French name of uncertain origins which may come from the Celtic 'white wave' or 'race' and 'woman'.

Georgia A feminine form of George, also the name of an American state.

Georgiana, Georgina Feminine forms of George. Diminutives are Georgie or Gina.

Geraldine Feminine form of Gerald. From the Old German for 'spear maiden'.

Germaine From the French for 'woman from Germany'. Used in various English-speaking countries, made famous by feminist writer and academic Germaine Greer.

Gilberta Feminine form of Gilbert. From the Old German for 'bright will'. Gigi is a diminutive.

Gilda Celtic name meaning 'god's servant'.

Gillian, Jillian The English form of Juliana ('from the Julius family'). Popular in the Middle Ages. The 'G' spelling is the earlier form and less common today. Short forms Gill and Jill.

Gina Originally a pet form of names ending in 'gina', for example, Georgina, Regina, now also used as an independent name.

Gisela From the Old German for 'a promise'. Also Gisella. The French form is Giselle.

Giselle French form of Gisela.

Giuletta Italian form of Juliet.

Glenda A Welsh name meaning 'from the glen'.

Glenys A Welsh name meaning 'holy'. Also Glenice, Glenis.

Gloria From the Latin for 'fame, glory'.

Grace From the Latin for 'grace'. Virtue name adopted by the Puritans in the seventeenth century. Pet form is Gracie.

Griselda From the Old German for 'grey battle maiden'.

Gudrun Norse for 'divine wisdom'.

Gwen, Gwenda A diminutive of Gwendoline.

Gwendoline From the Welsh, meaning 'white circle', possibly a reference to the moon. The name of Merlin's wife. Short forms are Gwen and Gwenda.

Gwyneth From the Welsh, meaning 'happiness' or 'blessed'. Gwynedd is the name of a county in northern Wales. Its diminutive is Gwyn. Also Gwynneth.

H

Habeeba, Habibah Arabic name meaning 'beloved'.

Hadassah Jewish biblical name meaning 'myrtle'.

Hannah, Hanna A popular biblical name, it is an

abbreviated form of the Hebrew 'Hanani', meaning 'God has favoured me', often shortened to 'favour' or 'grace'. Hannah was the name of the mother of Samuel the prophet. The name spread throughout Europe as the Greek form 'Anna', so Anne and all its variants are related forms. It began to be popular as 'Hannah' in Europe in the seventeenth century. The many variants include Scandinavian Hanne; the Czechoslovakian Hana, Hanicka and Hanka; and the Estonian Hanni. Pet forms include Hanne, Hannie and Hanny. See also Ann.

Harriet   Generally regarded as a feminine form of Harry. Also a variant of Henrietta.

Haruko   Japanese name meaning 'spring'.

Haseena, Hasina   An Arabic name meaning 'beautiful'.

Hayley, Haley, Hailey   From the Old English, meaning 'hay meadow'; a placename, surname and a personal name. Hayley Lewis is a champion Australian swimmer.

Hazel   A plant name, from the tree which bears nuts of the same name. A number of flower and plant names came to be popular as personal names in Britain in the late nineteenth century.

Heather   A Scottish botanical name, used since the end of the nineteenth century. The masculine form is Heath.

Hebe   A Greek name meaning 'youth'. Hebe, daughter of Zeus and Hera, was a cupbearer to the Greek gods.

Hedda   From the Old German, meaning 'struggle' or 'war'. An 1890 play by Norwegian dramatist Henrik Ibsen was titled *Hedda Gabler*. German forms are Heda and Hede.

Heidi   The name evolved from a diminutive of the

German 'Adelheid' (see 'Adelaide'). The enduring children's story of this name by Johanna Spry was first published in 1881 and helped to popularise the name.

Helen The Greek Helene is the feminine of Helenos, 'the bright one'. Helen, said to be the most beautiful woman in the world, was carried to Troy by Paris, and the Trojan War ensued. She was thus said by poet Christopher Marlowe to have 'the face that launched a thousand ships'. In the fourth century St Helen (or Helena), who it was said was the daughter of the British king 'Old King Cole', was the mother of Roman Emperor Constantine; her cult made the name popular in Britain. For many years there the usual form of the name was the variant Ellen. English variants include Helena, Helene, Elaine and possibly Eleanor. Diminutives include Nell, Nellie, Nelly. Other forms include the French Hélène; the Russian Yelena, Olena, Galina, Galinka, Alenka; the Polish Helenka, Helka and Hela; the Czechoslovakian Lenka, Jelena and Alena; and the Greek Eleni and Elli.

Helena English French and Spanish form of Helen.

Helene A variant of Helen, derived from the French form of the name.

Helenka Polish form of Helen.

Helga A Norse name meaning 'holy', found in Scandinavia.

Héloise French variant of Louise.

Henna Variant of Hannah, and also a deep orange-red powder from the leaves of the henna plant, used as a dye.

Henrietta From Henriette, the French feminine form of Henry. Harriet is a variant, and among its diminutes are Etta, Ettie, Etty, Henny and Hetty.

Hermione   The feminine form of the Greek 'Hermes', the messenger of the Gods.

Hillary, Hilary   From the Latin *hilarius*. It means 'cheerful, merry', and is used for both boys and girls.

Hoa   A Vietnamese name meaning 'flower'.

Holly   From the plant, whose name comes from the Anglo-Saxon 'holy', due to the traditional association with Christmas.

Hope   Anglo-Saxon virtue name that was popular with the Puritans. The name of one of the three daughters of St Sophia in the early Christian era, the other two being Faith and Charity.

Hoshiko   A Japanese girls' name meaning 'star'.

Hrisoula   Greek girls' name, with variant Soula.

Hypatia   From the Greek *hypatos*, meaning 'highest'. Hypatia was the first woman to teach philosophy and mathematics, and was put to death by a mob of Christians in the fifth century.

I

Ianthe   This is the Greek name for 'violet-coloured flower'. The nineteenth-century Romantic poet Shelley named his daughter Ianthe. Iolanthe is a related name.

Ida   A name of disputed Teutonic origins. A Norman introduction to Britain at the time of the Norman Conquest. Welsh variant Idelle, German variant Idette.

Ilana   A Hebrew name meaning 'a large tree'. Popular in Israel.

Ilona   A Hungarian form of Helen.

Ilsa, Ilse   Variants of Elsa or Elizabeth, they were initially German pet forms of the name.

Imagina   The name of the Duchess of Luxembourg in 1400. Related to Imogen.

Iman   Muslim name meaning 'believer, faithful'.

Imelda   An Italian name from the Old German for 'pervasive warfare' or 'strong battler'. Imelda Marcos is the well-heeled wife of the late President Marcos of the Philippines.

Imogen   First appearing as the name of a Shakespearean heroine in *Cymbeline*, it may have been a misprint for Innogen, which in turn may have come from the Old Irish for 'daughter' or 'girl'.

India   A personal name after the country. Lord Mountbatten, the last viceroy of India, called his grand-daughter after the country. May be used as a short form for Indiana.

Indiana   After the American state. Also used for males.

Indigo   From the Latin, after the deep blue colour.

Indira   A Hindu Sanskrit name. Indira was one of the names of Lakshmi, married to Vishnu, who was the goddess of heaven and thunderstorms. Indira Ghandi was India's first woman Prime Minister.

Indu   A Hindu name meaning 'moon'.

Inessa   A Russian name. The diminutive is Inka.

Inez, Inés   Spanish forms of Agnes.

Inga, Inge   Short forms of the Scandinavian Ingeborg, often used in their own right. Ingeborg comes from the Old Norse for 'Ing's protection'. Ing was a Norse god of fertility, abundance and peace.

Ingrid   Another Norse name relating to Ing (god of fertility abundance and peace), meaning 'Ing's ride'. Ingrid Bergman was an actor.

Io   According to Greek mythology, Io was a princess loved by Zeus, who turned her into a heifer to hide her from the jealousy of another goddess.

Ioanna Greek name for girls.

Iola From the Greek for 'violet coloured' or 'dawn mist'.

Iolanthe Greek name meaning 'violet-coloured flower'. Associated names are Yolande and Violet.

Iona A placename. Iona is an island of the Hebrides off the coast of Mull, Argyll in Scotland.

Iphigenia Agamemnon and Clytemnestra's daughter, according to Greek mythology.

Iram Arabic name for girls meaning 'heaven'.

Irena Slavic form of Irene. Czechoslovakian diminutives include Irenka and Irka.

Irene From the Greek word meaning 'peace'. In ancient Greece Eirene was the goddess of peace and one of the Horae ('the hours', the three goddess daughters of Zeus and Themis associated with nature and fertility). The 'e' was traditionally pronounced in England, after the Greek pronunciation, but has now mainly been replaced by the American two-syllable pronunciation. Variations include Eirena, Romanian and Russian Irina, and Polish and Czechoslovakian Irena. Also Romanian Irini. Pet forms Rene, Rena and Renie are also used in their own right.

Irina Romanian and Russian form of Irene.

Irini Romanian variant of Irene.

Iris From the Greek for 'the rainbow'. Iris was a Greek goddess who was the personification of the rainbow and a messenger of the gods. The name was given to the flower, which comes in many colours.

Isa A pet form of Isabel, found in Scotland as an independent name. Another derivation of this name is from the Old German for 'iron'.

Isabel, Isabelle, Isabella   A variant of Elizabeth which
  may have come from Provence. Belle, Bella and Isa
  are pet forms, also Issy and Izzy. Isobel, Isbel,
  Iseabel and Ishbel are Scottish forms. Other variants
  include the French Isabeau; the Polish Izabellà; and
  the Portuguese Isabelhina.

Isadora   From the Greek 'gift of Isis'. Isis was the
  Egyptian god of fertility and nature. Isadora
  Duncan was an avant-garde American dancer who
  was strangled with her own scarf when it got
  caught in her car wheels. A less common male
  form is Isidore.

Isis   Isis was the Egyptian goddess of fertility and
  nature. She was the wife of Osiris and the mother of
  Horus.

Isla   A name of uncertain origin, it may be from the
  Greek for 'from the island'. Also the name of a
  Scottish river.

Isobel   A Scottish form of Isabel.

Isolde, Isolda   There is disagreement as to whether
  this name has Welsh (meaning 'beautiful') or
  German (meaning 'icy rule') origins. According to
  the legend Isolde, the Irish King's daughter, had a
  love affair with Tristan. Also Yseulte, Iseult.

Issy, Izzy   Diminutives of names beginning with 'Is'
  such as Isabel or Isodora.

Ita   Irish name, from the Latin for 'thirst'. Ita Buttrose
  is a well-known media figure in Australia.

Ithaca   A placename; Ithaca is a Greek island.

Ivana, Ivanna   Slavic form of Jane or Joanna, meaning
  'god is gracious'.

Ivette   A French name; an alternative of Yvette and
  Evette.

Ivy   From the vine, apparently signifying
  'faithfulness'. Like some other plant names only in

use as a personal name since the late nineteenth century.

Izora Arabic name meaning 'dawn'.

Izumi Japanese name meaning 'fountain'.

Izzy See Issy.

J

Jacinta A Spanish name, meaning 'hyacinth'. According to Greek myth, Apollo made this flower spring from the blood of the dead Hyacinthus, a beautiful youth. French forms are Hyacinthe and Jacinthe; the Italian is Giacinta.

Jackie, Jacqui, Jacquie, Jacky Diminutives of Jacqueline.

Jacqueline A feminine short form of Jacques, which is a French name for boys equated with James and Jacob ('the supplanter'). Also Jaclyn, Jacquelyn and many other spellings. See also Jacques.

Jade After the green precious stone.

Jaleela Arabic name meaning 'honour, distinction'.

Jamila, Jamilla, Jameela, Djamila Arabic name meaning 'elegant and attractive'.

Jamie, Jaime The diminutive of James, the boys' name, from the Hebrew meaning 'the supplanter'. Also Jami, Jaimy, Jaimee.

Jan A diminutive of Janet, Janice or Janine. Also a boys' name.

Jane, Jayne One of the many feminine forms of John, which evolved via the Hebrew Johanna (meaning 'God is gracious' or 'Jehovah has favoured') and the French form Jehane. Appeared in Britain from the sixteenth century when Jane Seymour became the third wife of Henry VIII. Short forms are Janie, Jaynie. There are numerous variants, including Jan, Jana, Janeen, Janina, Janine, Janice, Jean, Jeanette, Jeanine, Joan, Joanna, Jo Ann, Johanna, Johanne, the Scottish Gaelic Sine, Sheena and Shena, Sinead and Siobhan. Spanish forms are Juanita and Juana; Italian Giovanna; and Slavic Jana.

Janet   Feminine form of John, originally a diminutive of Jane. Variants are Janetta and Janette; diminutives Jan, Jennie, Jenny and Jessie.

Janice   A variant form of Jane. Also spelt Janis.

Janine   Variant form of Jane. Also Janene, Jannine and Jannina.

Jasmin, Jasmine   From the Persian name for the fragrant-smelling flower. Also Jazmin, Jasmina, Jessamine and Yasmin.

Jayne   See Jane.

Jazz   After the type of music.

Jean   A feminine form of John, from the Old French name Jehane. Diminutives are Jeanette, Jeanie, Jeannette and Jeannie.

Jeanne   The French feminine form of John, derived from the Old French name Jehane, the French equivalent of Jane, Jean or Joan. Jeanne d'Arc was burnt at the stake for heresy in 1431.

Jemima   Sources differ as to the meaning of this name. Some say that it comes from the Hebrew for 'dove', and others from the Hebrew for 'right-handed'. Short forms are Jemmie, Jemma and Jem.

Jenna   A variant of Jenny.

Jenny, Jennie   Diminutives of Jennifer.

Jennifer   From the Old Welsh for 'white wave'. It evolved from the Cornish form Guenevere or

Guinevere. Also Jenifer, Gennifer. Short forms Jen, Jenny, Jennie, Jenna, Jenni.

Jerry, Jerrie, Jeri, Gerry, Geri Diminutives of Geraldine, also used as independent names.

Jessica From the Hebrew, meaning 'He beholds' or 'God Beholds'. The name was used by Shakespeare in *The Merchant of Venice* for Shylock's daughter. Short forms Jess, Jessie, Jesse. The Italian form is Gessica and the Polish form is Czeslawa.

Jessie, Jesse Short form of Jessica or Jessamine, sometimes used as names in their own right.

Jill, Jillian See Gillian.

Jill, Jilly, Jillie, Gill, Gilly, Gillie Diminutives of Jillian and Gillian.

Jitka A Czechoslovakian name for girls.

Jo A diminutive of Joanna, Joanne or Josephine, sometimes used as a name in its own right.

Joan A feminine form of John, derived from the Latin name Johanna. Famous bearers of the name include the French heroine Joan of Arc (Jeanne d'Arc). Siobhan is a variant.

Joanna A feminine form of John, derived from the Latin name Johanna. Joanne is a variant (also the French), and the diminutive is Jo.

Jocelyn From the Latin *jocunda*, meaning 'jocund, cheerful'.

Jodie, Jody, Jodi Originally short forms of Judith, now names in their own right.

Joelle, Joella Probably from the Hebrew, meaning 'Jehovah is God'; feminine forms of Joel.

Johanna A feminine form of John. See Jane, Joan, Joanna, Joanne.

Jordan From the Hebrew, meaning 'descending'.

Josephine The name is a feminine form of Joseph, which means 'Jehovah adds' (referring to family

additions). The pet form is Josie, Polish form
Jozefina and Spanish form Josefina.

Josefina   Spanish form of Josephine.

Joy   As in 'delight'. A name taken up in the
seventeenth century by the Puritans.

Joyce   Latin for 'joyous'. See also Jocelyn and Joy.

Jozefina   Polish form of Josephine.

Juanita   Spanish form of Joan.

Jude, Judy   Short forms of Judith.

Judith   Meaning literally 'woman from Judea', referring
to 'a Jewish woman'. Pet forms include Jude, Judy,
Judie. The French form is Judithe; the Italian Giuda;
the Hungarian Judit, Juci, Jucika and Jutka; the
Italian Giuditta; the Hebrew Yehudit; and the Latvian
Judite.

Julia, Julie   Feminine forms of Julius (after the Roman
clan name of Julius Caesar), which meant 'soft-
haired, downy'. Julia is popular in America and
many European countries. Julie is the French form.
Polish forms are Jula, Julcia, Juleczka; the Russian
forms are Yuliya, Yulichka and Yulinka; and the
Romanian Iulia.

Juliana   A feminine form of Julian, borne by the
Christian martyr St Juliana. Liana is a short form.
Julienne is a related form.

Juliet   Diminutive form of Julia. Very strongly
associated with Juliet Capulet. The Italian form is
Giulietta; the Portuguese Julieta; and the Spanish
Julietta.

Julieta   Portuguese form of Juliet.

Juno   A variant of Una. Juno was a Roman goddess.

Justine, Justina   From the Latin for 'just'; feminine
forms of Justin. Justine is the more popular French
form.

Jutta   From the Old German, meaning 'war'.

K

Kacie, Kacey, KC   Alternative forms of Casey.

Kady, Cady, KD   Alternative forms of Katie. Also Kadie, Kadee, Cadie, Cadee.

Karen, Karin   Karen was initally a short form of Katarina used in Denmark. Danish immigrants introduced it to America. Variants are Karron, Karyn, Carin and Caren.

Karina   See Carina.

Karla   See Carla.

Kasey   See Casey.

Kate   A short form of Katherine, also a name in its own right.

Katherine   See Catherine.

Kathleen   See Catherine.

Katinka   A Russian form of Katherine.

Katrina   Anglicisation of Catriona.

Katya   A Russian form of Katherine.

Kay   A diminutive of Katherine or Kathleen. Often used as a name in its own right.

Kaz   A short form of Karen that is now used in its own right. Kaz Cooke is an Australian cartoonist and writer.

Keely, Keeley   Variants of Kelly.

Keiko   Japanese name meaning 'blessing'.

Kelila, Kelilah   From the Hebrew for 'garland', 'laurels'.

Kelly, Kelli, Kellie, Kellye   An Irish Gaelic name which probably means 'warrior'. A common surname used as a personal name for boys or girls. Its many variants include various forms of 'Keeley' and names that approximate 'Kylie'.

Kelsey   A placename from England, or from the

Scandinavian, meaning 'from the ship island'.

Kenya From the name of the country.

Keren A diminutive of the Hebrew name
Kerenhappuch (meaning 'horn of antimony',
referring to a cosmetic).

Kerry, Kerrie, Kerri A placename, after the Irish
county, meaning 'descendants of Ciar'. Also used
for boys.

Keshia An African name meaning 'favourite, most
beloved'.

Kezia, Keziah, Ketziah A Hebrew name meaning
'cassia', a cinammon-like spice used in incence
offerings. Keziah was one of Job's daughters. A
short form is Kezi.

Kia An African name meaning 'beginning of the
season'.

Kikuko Japanese name for girls meaning
'chrysanthemum'.

Kim A diminutive of Kimberley.

Kimberley, Kimberly, Kimberlea From a placename and
surname of disputed origins. It is closely associated
with the South African city and its diamond mines.
Also a boys' name.

Kingsley A placename meaning 'king's lea' or 'king's
meadow'. Also a boys' name.

Kira A name from the former Persia, meaning
'sun'.

Kirby From the Old Norse, meaning 'church village'.
A placename, surname, boys' name and now girls'
name.

Kirmi A Sanskrit Hindu name meaning 'golden
image'.

Kirsten The Scandinavian form of Christine. The
diminutive is Kirsty.

Kirsty A variant of Christina, or diminutive of Kirsten.

Kitty   Diminutive of Christine.

Kiyoko   Japanese name meaning 'cleanliness'.

Kristen, Kristin   Scandinavian forms of Christina and Christine.

Kristina, Kristine   See Christine.

Krystal   A spelling variation of Crystal.

Kylie   An Australian name, from an Aboriginal word meaning 'boomerang'.

Kyna   A Welsh name meaning 'wise'.

L

Lala   A Slovakian name that means 'tulip'. Also the name of a nymph who lost her tongue in Roman mythology.

Lana   May be a diminutive of Alana.

Laraine, Larraine   Variants of Lorraine.

Larissa   Of uncertain origin, possibly Russian, or from the Latin *hilaris*, meaning 'cheerful', or a Greek placename meaning 'citadel'.

Lateefah   Muslim name that is popular in the north of Africa.

Laura   Probably from the Latin *laurus*, meaning 'laurel'. The laurel is a small evergreen, whose leaves are used for cooking. Wreaths of its leaves were used to honour sporting heroes and scholars in ancient Rome and Greece. Variants are Lauraine, Laureen, Lauren, Lauretta, Loreen, Loren, Loretta and Lorinda. Diminutives include Lauri, Laurie and Lori. Laurel is a related name.

Lauren   See Laura.

Laurentia, Laurencia   Feminine forms of Laurence.

Leah   A Hebrew name meaning 'cow' or 'weary one'. Biblical name of Jacob's first wife.

Leanne   Compound of 'Lee' and 'Anne'.

Lee, Leigh, Lea   Used for both sexes, another name that has evolved from a surname, from the Old English *leah*, meaning 'meadow, lea'.

Leila   A name from Persia meaning 'dark'. Also Leilah, Lela.

Lena   A short form of Helena.

Leni   A German form of Helen.

Lenore   A variant of Eleanor.

Leonie   A French name which is the feminine form of Leon, meaning 'lion'. Also Leona.

Leonora   From a variant of Eleanor. Diminutives include Nora and Norah.

Lesley   After a Scottish placename and surname. Leslie is the masculine form.

Libby   A diminutive of Elizabeth.

Liddy   A diminutive of Lydia.

Lila   See Leila.

Lydia   From the Greek, meaning 'woman of Lydia' (Asia Minor).

Lilian, Lillian   Either from the Latin *lilium*, 'lily', or a diminutive of Elizabeth. Variants are Lilias, Lillias, Lillie and Lily.

Lilith   In Jewish folklore, a female demon believed to be the first wife of Adam, her name coming to mean 'storm goddess'.

Lilka   A Polish form of Louise.

Lily   Variant of Lilian, and also influenced by the flower lily, which is a symbol of purity.

Lina   A diminutive of Carolina. Also a name in its own right.

Linda, Lynda   Derived from the Old German *lindi* for serpent, symbolic of wisdom. Linda is also a Xhosa name from South Africa which means 'wait'. The diminutive is Lindy.

Lindsay From a Scottish surname and placename. The feminine form is usually spelt Lindsey or Lynsey.

Lindy Diminutive of Linda.

Linnet See Lynette.

Lisa A diminutive of Elizabeth that is popular in its own right. For the Fon of Togo and Southern Benin, Lisa is the name of the sun god of creation, who takes the form of a chameleon. Also Liza.

Lisbeth A diminutive of Elizabeth, often used as a name in its own right.

Lise A German diminutive of Elizabeth.

Lisette A French diminutive of Elizabeth.

Liza A diminutive of Elizabeth and Eliza, often used as a name in its own right.

Lola Short form of Carlotta and Dolores, used as a name in its own right.

Lolita A diminutive of Dolores, often used as a name in its own right. Also the heroine of one of Vladimir Nabokov's novels.

Loren See Lauren.

Lorna From the name of a Scottish chieftain, also a placename. The masculine form is Lorne.

Lorraine From the name of a region in France, meaning 'Lothair's kingdom'. Variants are Laraine, Laraine, Lauraine and Loraine.

Louisa French feminine form of Louis. Short forms are Lou and Lulu.

Louise French feminine form of Louis. Many short forms, including Lou, Louie, Lu and Lulu. Variants include Aloise, Eloise, Eloisa, Heloise, the Polish Lilka, Ludka, Ludwika and Luisa, the Slovian Luiza, the German Aloisa and Luise, and Greek Eloisia. Combined forms include Cindy-Lou and Marylou.

Loveday   An old Cornish name, originally given to children born on a loveday.

Lucia   The feminine form of Lucius, now regarded the Italian form of Lucy. St Lucia was martyred in the fourth century. Anglicised forms included Lucy and Luce. Variants are Lucetta, Lucette, Lucilla, Lucinda and Lucy.

Luciana, Lucienne   Feminine forms of Lucian.

Lucie   The French form of Lucia.

Lucilla   A variant of Lucia, borne by a Roman martyr of the third century.

Lucille   The French form of Lucilla.

Lucinda   A seventeenth-century variation of Lucy.

Lucy   From the Latin *lux*, meaning 'light'. Variants include Lucia, Lucienne, Lucille and Lucinda.

Luisa   A Polish form of Louise.

Lulu   A diminutive of Louisa, Louise and Lucy.

Lydia   From the Greek, meaning 'woman of Lydia', a region of Asia Minor.

Lyn, Lynne, Lynn, Lin   Short forms of Lynette or Linda.

Lynette, Linette   From the Old French for 'a linnett bird'. It originally came from the Latin for flax, on which the linnett feeds. Short forms Lyn, Lynne, Lin. Variants Linetta, Linette, Lynnette.

Lynsey   See Lindsay.

Lyra   From the Greek for 'lyre'.

M

Mabel   From the Latin, meaning 'lovable'.

Madeline, Madeleine, Madelaine   The original form is Magdalene, meaning 'woman of Magdala', birthplace of St Mary Magdalene, the patron saint of penitents, on the Sea of Galilee. Madeline is the French form. A common pet form is Maddie or Maddy, and the many variants include Magda (found in a number of countries), the Czechoslovakian Magdalena; the French Magdalaine and Madelon; the Greek Magdalini; the Italian Maddalena; and the Irish Maighlin.

Maddison, Madison An English surname that is being used as a girls' first name as well as for boys. It may mean 'son of Maude' or 'son of the strong warrior'.

Madonna From the Italian for 'my lady'. The Virgin Mary is referred to as the Madonna.

Mae See May.

Maeve This name is an Anglicised form of Meadhbh, who was a legendary Irish fairy queen, also referred to as Mab or Maud. Variants of the name are Mave and Meave.

Magda Diminutive of Magdalene, a reference to Mary Magdalene. See Madeleine.

Maggie Diminutive of Margaret, used as a name in its own right.

Mahala A Hebrew name that means 'tenderness'. Variants are Mahalah and Mahalia.

Mair Welsh form of Mary.

Maire An Irish name derived from Mary (or Maria). From the diminutive Mairin both 'Maura' and 'Maureen' were developed. Moira (also Moyra) is the anglicised form of Maire.

Maisie A Scottish familiar form of Margaret, which is also used as a name in its own right.

Malai A Scottish form of Molly.

Mali A Thai name meaning 'jasmine'.

Mallory, Malory A surname from the Old French for 'unlucky', used as a personal name for either sex.

Mandy, Mandie   Diminutives of Amanda.

Manuela   A Spanish name from the Hebrew for 'God is with us'. The feminine form of Emmanuel. A diminutive is Manuelita.

Mara, Marah   Hebrew biblical name meaning 'bitter'. Possibly the word from which Mary was derived. Mara is also a Czechoslovakian short form of Tamara.

Marcia   From the Latin for 'warlike', relating to Mars, Roman god of war. Marsha is derived from Marcia and other forms are Marcella, Marcellina and the French Marceline. Diminutives Marci, Marcie and Marcy have been used independently.

Mardi   From the French for Tuesday.

Mare, Maire   Irish form of Mary.

Margaret   This classic name is probably derived from the Greek for 'pearl', although some sources believe it to be of Persian derivation, meaning 'child of light'. The name was one of the most frequently found girls' names in the Middle Ages, and has also been very popular in the nineteenth and twentieth centuries. Variants include Margaretta, Margarita, Margherita, Margherite, Marguetta, Marguerite, Marjorie, Margery, Margred, Margo and Margot. Pet forms include Madge, Maggie, Meg, Maisie, Maggie, Greta, Gretel, Peg, Peggy and Rita. German forms include Margarethe, Gretchen, Grethel and Marghet; Danish Margarete, Mette and Maret; Slavonic Marjarita and Marjeta; and Lithuanian Magryta.

Margot, Margo   French diminutive of Margaret used as a name in its own right. Dame Margot Fonteyn was a famous English prima ballerina.

Mari   Japanese name for girls, meaning 'truth'.

Maria   The Latin form of Mary. The usual form of the

name in Germany, Italy, Spain and a number of
other European countries.

Marian, Marianne, Mary Anne   Variants of Marion.

Marie   A French variant of Mary, also an early form
of the name in England.

Marielle   A French name for girls.

Marilyn   A variant of Mary. Also spelt Merilyn and
Merrilyn.

Marina   The derivation is uncertain, but it may be
from the Latin *marinus*, meaning 'from the sea'.

Marion   A French form of Mary, originally a
diminutive of Marie, which was bought to England
by the Normans. Led to variants Marian, Marianne
and Mary Anne.

Marisa, Marissa, Marita   Variants of Mary.

Marnie   A name of uncertain origins, possibly a
variant derived from Marina.

Marsha   A form of Marcia.

Martina   Feminine form of Martin (from the Latin for
'warlike', after Mars, the Roman god of war).

Mary   A biblical name associated with the Virgin
Mary, it was too much revered until the twelfth
century to be used as a personal name. However it
became the most common name for girls in England
for much of the sixteenth to nineteenth centuries,
and was equally popular in the forms Maria and
Marie in other countries. The name's origins are
unclear, and various derivations are suggested: that
it is an Egyptian name derived from 'meri Amen',
and that it has Hebrew derivations concerned with
'the sea', 'rebellion' or a 'wanted child'. It was first
translated as 'Miriam', and may be related to Mara,
from the Hebrew *marah*, meaning 'bitterness'.
Many diminutives were created to distinguish
between all the 'Marys', for instance, May, Molly,

Polly and the Scottish Minnie. The Irish name was Maire, from which many other names developed. The traditional Welsh form is Mair. Variants include Marie, Maria, Mair, Mariel, Marietta, Marian, Marianne, Marion, Marilyn, Marla, Maura, Maureen, Maryse, Moira and Moyra.

Masumi   Japanese name meaning 'beauty'.

Matilda   From the Old High German meaning 'mighty battlemaid'. Also Mathilda; short forms Matty, Tilly.

Maureen   Derived from Mairin, a diminutive of Maire, an Irish form of Mary.

Maxie   Short form of Maxine.

Maxine   Feminine form of Maximilian, or Max, from the Latin *maximus*, meaning 'the greatest'. Short form Maxie, variant Maxina.

May   A diminutive of Mary or Margaret, also a name in its own right. Mae was popularised by the American actress Mae West.

Meg   Short form of Margaret.

Megan, Meghan, Meagan   Welsh variants of Margaret.

Meihua   Chinese name which means 'beautiful flower'.

Mei Mei   Chinese name meaning 'beautiful, beautiful'.

Melania   Italian form of Melanie.

Melanie   From the Greek for 'dark' or 'black'. The name became fashionable after the publication of Margaret Mitchell's *Gone with the Wind*. Many variants, including Melany, Melloney, Melonie and Melaine. Italian form Melania.

Melba   From the Latin, meaning 'mallow flower', or the Greek, 'soft, slender'. Nellie Melba was an opera singer.

Melinda   Compound of Melanie and Linda.

Melissa From the Greek, meaning 'honey' or 'honey-bee'. Also the name of a herb. Short forms are Lissa and Mel.

Melody, Melodie From the Greek word for 'song'.

Mercedes From the Spanish for mercy, which led to 'Maria de las Mercedes', a title of the Virgin Mary. Also the name of a car.

Meredith Derived from the Welsh name Maredudd, meaning 'great chief of the sea'. Diminutive is Merry.

Mia Modern short form of Michaela, and diminutive of Maria.

Michaela, Mikayla, Mikaela A feminine form of Michael (from the Hebrew for 'who is like God?'). Another variant is Makayla; a short form is Mia.

Michelle Also Michele. Feminine forms of Michael.

Midori Japanese name for girls meaning 'green'.

Mignon French name meaning 'darling, favourite'.

Mikayla See Michaela.

Milly, Millie Short forms of Emily, Camilla and Camille.

Mima Familiar form of Jemima.

Mimi A diminutive of Mary, also used as an independent name.

Minerva Roman goddess of wisdom, arts and crafts.

Minna, Mina A name which may be derived from a diminutive of Wilhelmina (a German feminine of William).

Minnie A Scottish diminutive of Mary, and also of Wilhelmina (a German feminine of William).

Mira Possibly a short form of Mirabel or Miranda, or an alternative form of Myra, meaning wonderful.

Mirabel, Mirabelle From the Latin for 'wonderful, amazing'.

Miranda Latin for 'worthy of admiration'. Said to be a Shakespearean creation for the heroine of the

romantic drama *The Tempest*. An Australian literary
Miranda is the schoolgirl who disappeared in Joan
Lindsay's *Picnic at Hanging Rock*.

Miriam   From the Hebrew, meaning 'bitter'. The
original Hebrew form of Mary.

Moira, Moyra   See Maire.

Molly   Short form of Mary. A Scottish form is Malai.

Mona   From the Irish name Muadhnait, meaning
'noble'. Also associated with the name of Leonardo
da Vinci's portrait, *Mona Lisa* (La Gioconda in
Europe).

Monica   A name of uncertain etymology, possibly
from the Latin for 'advise', or the Greek, meaning
'alone'. St Monica, the mother of St Augustine, was
from Africa. The French form is Monique, the
German Monika.

Morag   From the Scottish Gaelic, meaning 'great' or
'sun'.

Morgan   An Old Welsh name, usually held to mean
'sea bright'. A surname, it was traditionally used
mainly for boys as a personal name. Morgana,
which is sometimes found, is also an Arabic name.

Muriel   Of disputed origins, but may be from the
Celtic for 'sea bright', as Morgan is held to be. The
Normans brought the name to Britain. Miriel,
Meriall and Meryall are variants. Merle, Meryl and
Merrill may have derived from Meriel.

Murphy   An Irish surname, now used as a personal
name.

Myfanwy, Myvanwy   A Welsh name meaning 'my fine
one'.

Myra, Mira   Said to be a literary invention of Fulke
Greville, Lord Brooke, for the subject of a love poem.
According to Greek mythology, the mother of Adonis
was called Myrrha. The spelling alternative is Mira.

N

Nada   A variant of Nadia.

Nadia   A Slavic diminutive from the name Nadezhda, meaning 'hope'. The name is popular in Russia: Vladimir Lenin's wife was called Nadia. Associated forms are Nada, Nadya and Nadka. Nadine is a French form.

Nadine   French form of Nadia, which has been used since the nineteenth century in English-speaking countries. Nadine Gordimer is a South African writer.

Nancy   Its history is as a pet form of Anne (from the Hebrew 'grace' or 'favour'), which has been regarded as a name in its own right for many years. Diminutives Nan, Nancy, Nanette.

Nanette   A variant of Ann.

Naida   According to Greek mythology the *naiads* were fresh water nymphs found in rivers, streams and fountains. Also Naia, Naiad.

Naomh   An Irish name meaning 'saint'.

Naomi   From the Hebrew, meaning 'pleasant'. According to the Old Testament, Naomi, wife of Elimelech, was Ruth's mother-in-law, who went to live in a place called Moab to escape lean times in Bethlehem. The name was adopted by the Puritans in England in the seventeenth century, and is popular in Australia. Variants Naoma, Naomie.

Nara   Various derivations given, including the Old English for 'near one, close one'.

Narcissus   From the Greek for 'daffodil'. In Greek myth Echo loved the beautiful youth Narcissus, who did not reciprocate. Echo pined away, and Artemis

154

punished Narcissus by making him fall in love with his own reflection in a pool. Narcissa is an alternative feminine form and Narcisse is the masculine form.

Nastasia, Nastassja Variant Russian forms of Anastasia (from the Greek for 'resurrection').

Natalie, Natalia From the Latin *natalis* for 'Christmas'. Natalia (Natalya) is a popular Russian form and the name Natasha is actually its diminutive. Other diminutives are Natalka, Natashenka, Talya, Tasha, Tashka and Tasya. A Spanish variant is Natacha.

Natasha A diminutive of the Russian Natalia (Natalya), it is now used in its own right.

Natsuyo Japanese name meaning 'summer'.

Neala, Neila, Neela An Irish Gaelic name which is a feminine form of Neal, Neil ('champion').

Nell Short form of Ellen, Eleanor and Helen. Also Nellie, Nelly, Nelle.

Nerina Variant of Nerissa.

Nerissa The probable derivation is from the Greek name Nereid, meaning 'sea nymph'. Variant form Nerina.

Neroli, Nerolie From the Greek for 'orange blossom'. The name is associated with the oil distilled from flowers of the orange to make perfume. Also Nerolia.

Nerys A Welsh name meaning 'lord'.

Nevada From the Spanish for 'snow', and a name of one of the states in the US.

Niam, Niamh An Irish name meaning 'luminous'.

Nicola The Italian form of Nicole.

Nicole, Nichole A feminine form of Nicholas. Diminutives include Nicky, Nickie, Nikki, Niki.

Nicky, Nicki, Nikki, Niki Pet forms of Nichole, Nicola

or other 'Nic' names. Now likely to be used as names in their own right.

Nicolette An alternative French form of Nicole. The name Collette is actually a diminutive of this name that has become an independent name.

Nina Originally a Russian diminutive form of Anne, used in English-speaking countries since the nineteenth century. Also the Spanish word for 'girl'. French variants Ninon and Ninette.

Nita Juanita is a diminutive of the Spanish name Juana (Joan) and Nita is a short form of Juanita.

Noelle From the Latin *natalis*, Christmas, via the Old French 'noël'. Traditionally given to babies born on Christmas day since the Middle Ages, in the form Nowel in England and Noël in France. A variant is Noelene.

Nonie, Noni Pet forms of Nora and Leonie.

Nora, Norah Variants of Honour, Eleanor and Leonore, introduced into Ireland after the Norman Conquest.

Norma May derive from the Latin for 'a principle or rule'.

Nova From the Latin *novus*, meaning 'new'.

O

Obelia Greek name related to 'a marker' or 'a needle'.

Octavia Feminine form of Octavius, from the Latin for 'eighth'. French form Octavie.

Odessa From the Greek for 'long journey'. Placename after the port city in Russia.

Odette   French name of disputed origins, which may be from the German for 'prosperous, wealthy'.

Ola   Scandinavian feminine of Olaf.

Olga   Russian form of Helga, which is an Old Norse name meaning 'holy'. Other Russian forms include Olka, Olya and Olyusha.

Olivia   Latin name meaning 'olive'. The olive branch is a symbol of peace. It is said that a Roman virgin martyr called St Oliva was the patron of the olive-tree.

Ollie   Pet form of Olive and other 'Ol' names.

Olwen, Olwyn   Welsh name for girls, meaning 'white footprint'.

Olympia   Greek name meaning 'from Olympus, from the heavens'. According to Greek mythology the gods lived on Mount Olympus.

Ondrea   A Czechoslovakian form of Andrea.

Oni   A name from West Africa which means 'desired'.

Omega   From the Greek, meaning 'final, ultimate'. The last letter of the Greek alphabet.

Oona, Oonagh   See Una.

Opal   Hindu Sanskrit name meaning 'precious stone'.

Ophelia   From the Greek for 'aid or help'. Also the heroine of the early seventeenth-century Shakespearean tragedy *Hamlet* who is driven to insanity and drowns.

Oralie   French form of Aurelia.

Oriana   From the Latin via the Old French for 'to rise', implying sunrise, dawn.

Orla, Orlaith, Orlagh   An Irish name, meaning 'golden princess'.

P

Pachan   A name for boys or girls from Gambia meaning 'pampered pet'.

Pagan   From the Latin *paganus*, which means 'villager' or 'yokel' but also gained the meaning 'heathen'. It came to be used as a personal name and was brought to Britain by the Normans.

Page, Paige   An occupational name referring to a young attendant on a person of high order, such as a knight. It became a surname and is now used as a girls' name.

Paloma   Spanish name meaning 'dove'. Artist Pablo Picasso named his daughter Paloma.

Pamela   The literary creation of Sir Phillip Sydney for his 1590 romance *Arcadia*, possibly derived from the Greek for 'all honey'. The name was picked up in the eighteenth century by Samuel Richardson for his debut novel *Pamela*. Diminutives are Pam, Pammy.

Pandora   From the Greek word meaning 'all gifts'. Pandora, according to Greek mythology, was the first woman created by Hephaestus and Athene. She was sent by Zeus as a punishment for man, and her curiosity caused her to open 'Pandora's box', thereby releasing all human ills, hope alone remaining inside.

Paola   An Italian form of Paula.

Paris   After the city. According to Greek mythology, Hecuba, Paris' mother, dreamt while pregnant that she gave birth to a flaming firebrand. Paris was a Trojan prince whose seduction of Helen led to the Trojan War. The name has been used for both boys and girls.

Pascale A French name given to children born at Easter or Passover.

Pat Short form of Patricia.

Patience One of the abstract quality or 'virtue' names adopted by the Puritans after the Reformation.

Patrice A French form of Patricia.

Patricia After the Latin *patricius*, meaning 'aristocrat'. Found from the eighteenth century mainly in Scotland, until Queen Victoria's granddaughter Princess Patricia (Victoria Patricia Helena Elizabeth of Connaught) popularised the name. Short forms are Pat, Patty, Patti, Pattie, Patsy, Tricia and Trisha. The French form is Patrice, the Italian Patrizia.

Patrizia Italian form of Patricia.

Paula A feminine form of the Latin name Paul, from *paulus*, meaning 'small, little'. Italian variant Paola, Russian forms Pavla and Pawla.

Paulette A French feminine form of Paul ('small, little').

Paulina This is the feminine form of the Latin Paulinus, which is the diminutive of Paulus ('small, little'). Pauline has been the preferred form.

Pauline French feminine form of Paulina. Russian forms Pavia, Pavlina, Pavlinka.

Pavla Russian form of Paula.

Pavlina, Pavlinka Russian forms of Pauline.

Pax Greek for 'peace'.

Paz Spanish for 'peace'.

Pearl After the name of the jewel. Pearl S. Buck was a Nobel Prize-winning American writer. Also Pearle, Pearlie. Spanish form is Perla.

Peggy, Peggie Diminutives of Margaret (derived because Peggy rhymed with the variant Meggy). Also used in its own right. Short form is Peg. The Irish form is Peigi.

Peigi Irish form of Peggy.

Pela Polish diminutive of Penelopa (Penelope).

Pelagia A Greek name, meaning 'of the sea'.

Penelope From the Greek for 'weaver', or connected with 'a bobbin'. Penelope was the wife of Odysseus, a symbol of fidelity, who waited for him to return from Troy for a decade, keeping other suitors at bay. Short forms Penny, Pennie. Polish forms Penelopa, Pela, Pelcia, Lopa. The Greek short form is Popi.

Penina, Peninah Hebrew name for 'a pearl'. Short form Peni.

Pennie, Penny Diminutives of Penelope.

Perdita From the Latin for 'lost', created by Shakespeare for his play *A Winter's Tale*. Perdita is the 'lost' daughter of Leontes, king of Sicily and his wife Hermione.

Perrine A French name for girls.

Persephone In Greek mythology Persephone spent the fertile months with Demeter the corn goddess, and was thus the goddess of Spring and vegetation, but was forced to spend the other six barren months with Hades and so was queen of the underworld and symbolised death.

Persia After the country, now the Islamic Republic of Iran.

Pessia Israeli name for girls.

Peta A feminine form of Peter ('a rock').

Petra A feminine form of Peter ('a rock') and short form of Petronella. Also Petrina, Petrea.

Petronella A variant of the Latin Petronilla, which came from Petronius, a Roman clan name, itself derived from the Greek *petra*, a rock. French forms Pétronelle, Pétronille.

Pham Vietnamese name for girls.

Philippa, Phillippa Feminine forms of Phillip ('lover of horses'). Pet forms are Pippa and Pip. Italian forms are Filippa and Filippina.

Phoebe From the Greek for 'the shining or bright one'. Short form Fee. French variants are Photine and Phebe, Greek Photinee.

Phoenix In Egyptian mythology the phoenix was a bird which died every 500 years and then rose from the ashes of the funeral pyre. Also the capital of the American state of Arizona.

Pia From the Latin for 'devout, pious'.

Pilar Spanish name from the Latin, meaning 'pillar'. A reference to the Virgin Mary, the 'pillar' of the Christian Church.

Piper From the Old English for a player of bagpipes, a pipe or flute.

Pippa Diminutive of Phillippa or a name in its own right. Also Pip.

Polly A pet form for Mary, related to Molly, but now often used independently.

Poppy After the flower which symbolises peace.

Portia From the Latin, meaning 'offering'.

Prema Hindu name for girls meaning 'love'.

Priscilla From the Latin *priscus*, meaning 'former' or 'old-fashioned'. Pet forms Priss, Prissy or Cilla.

Prudence Another of the Puritan abstract quality or 'virtue' names. From the Latin for 'foresight, wisdom'. Short form Prue is heard more often.

Prue Diminutive of Prudence.

Psyche From the Greek, meaning 'soul'. Psyche was the soul personified, depicted sometimes as a butterfly. After many trials she was finally immortalised and united with Eros, the god of love.

Pua Hawai'ian name meaning 'flower'.

Q

Qamra   Arabic name meaning 'the moon'.

Queenie   This was often given as nickname for girls called 'Victoria' during the reign of Queen Victoria. It is also used for girls called 'Regina'.

Quentin, Quintan   For boys or girls, this name is from the Latin for 'the fifth child'. Feminine form Quintana is an alternative.

Querida   Spanish and Portuguese name meaning 'beloved'.

Quinn   From the Old English, meaning 'queen'.

Quyen   Female name from Vietnam.

R

Rachel   A perenially popular Biblical name from the Hebrew meaning 'ewe', innocence. According to Genesis the beautiful Rachel was the mother of Joseph. Variants include Rachael, Rachelle and Rachele, diminutives are Rach, Ray, Rae, Shell, Shelley. A German form is Rahel; the Bulgarian and Greek is Rahil; the Spanish and Portuguese is Raquel; and the Arabic is Raaheel. Rochelle may be a variant.

Rae, Ray   Diminutives of Rachel (or Raelene), also used independently.

Rafaela, Raffaella, Raphaela   The feminine form of Raphael (from the Hebrew meaning 'god has healed'). Short forms Raffi and Raff.

Raffi   Short form of Rafaela.

Raina, Raine, Rane   The origins are unclear. It may be a feminine form of Raynor, and it may come from the French word *reine* for queen; some sources suggest that it is related to *regina*, Latin for 'queen'. An alternative form is Reyna. The French forms Reine and Reinette may be related.

Ramona   The feminine form of Ramon, the Spanish form of Raymond.

Ramsey, Ramsay   A placename, Scottish surname and personal name, used for boys and now girls. From the Old English, meaning either 'ram's island', 'wild garlic island' or 'raven island'.

Rani   A Hindu name meaning 'queen'.

Raquel   Spanish and Portuguese form of Rachel.

Rasa   A Lithuanian name meaning 'dew'.

Raymonda   Feminine form of Raymond.

Reba   Diminutive of Rebecca.

Rebecca   A Hebrew name which may mean 'bound, noose', or 'heifer'. In the Old Testament Rebecca was Isaac's wife, the mother of Jacob and Esau. Daphne du Maurier wrote a novel called *Rebecca*, which was made into a film by Alfred Hitchcock in 1940. Also Rebeccah, Rebecka and pet forms Becc, Beck, Becky, Beckie, Becka and Reba. The French forms are Rebeque and Rebecque; the German Rebekke and Rebekka; the Bulgarian, Rumanian and Greek Reveka; the Hungarian and Slovakian Rebeka; and the Hebrew Rivka or Rivkah.

Regan, Reagan   A form of Regina ('queen' or 'noblewoman') which can be used as a name in its own right. Regan was the name of one of King Lear's three daughters.

Regina   A Latin word meaning 'queen' or 'noblewoman'. It became popular in Queen

Victoria's reign, as did Queenie. Variants include
Regena, Reginia and Regine.

Regine Variant of Regina.

Reiko Japanese name, meaning 'gratitude, prosperity'.

Renata From the Latin for 'born again' or 're-birth'.
The French variant is Renée. German and Latvian
variant Renate.

Rene, Renie Short forms of Irene.

Renée, René French forms of Renata (rebirth).

Reta A Finnish form of Rita.

Reveca A Bulgarian, Rumanian and Greek form of
Rebecca.

Rhea Rhea was a Greek goddess, the daughter of
Uranus and Gaea, and the mother of Zeus, who was
identified by the Greeks with the Anatolian nature
goddess Cybele. See also Ria.

Rhiannon Welsh name meaning 'nymph' or 'goddess',
or, according to some, 'witch'. Rhiannon featured in
the collection of tales of Celtic mythology called the
Mabinogion. Variants include Rhianna, Rhianon and
Rianon.

Rhoda A Greek name meaning 'rose'. The Latin
'Rhoda' actually meant 'woman from Rhodes', as its
beautiful roses were the reason for the naming of
the Greek Island 'Rhodes'. Also Roda.

Rhonda A placename from the river flowing through
the Rhondda Valley in southern Wales.

Ria Diminutive form of names with 'ria' endings such
as Victoria and Maria, also used as an independent
name. Also a Spanish name meaning 'river'. See
also Rhea.

Rica, Ricca Diminutive forms of names ending in
'rica', including Erica, Frederica and Ulrica.
Sometimes used as names in their own right.

Ricky, Rickie Diminutives of Frederica or similar

names. Also Ricki, Riki, Rikki and Rikky.

Riley, Reilly   Irish surname meaning 'valiant, courageous'.

Rita   Originally a diminutive of Margherita ('pearl'), it came to be used as an independent name. St Rita is the patron saint of Spoleto in Italy. Also Reta.

Rivka, Rivkah   Hebrew variants of Rebecca.

Roberta   Feminine form of Robert ('shining or bright fame').

Robin, Robyn   Derived from Robert ('shining or bright fame') via a diminutive of the nickname Rob, which was very common in the Middle Ages, and which began to be used for girls. Associated with a variety of small Australian and European birds. A variant is Robina.

Robina   Variant of Robin.

Rochelle   This name may be a variant of Rachel, or it may be from the French for 'little rock', as in the name of the Breton port.

Rodi   A Greek name for girls meaning 'pomegranate'.

Roesia   From the Old French, meaning 'rose'.

Rois, Roisin   An Irish name of disputed origins, it was brought to Britain by the Normans. May be a variant of the Latin *rosa* or derived from the Old German *hros* for horse.

Roma   A placename; the Italian word for Rome.

Romaine   From the French for a female Roman.

Rona   Possibly after the Scottish island of the same name.

Ronnie, Ronny   Diminutive of Veronica.

Rori, Rory   This name came from the Gaelic 'Ruairidh', which meant 'red'. A personal name for boys which has been taken up for girls.

Rosabella   A combination of Rose and Belle from the eighteenth century.

Rosaleen   An Irish form of Rose.

Rosalia, Rosalie   From the Latin *rosa*. St Rosalie is patron saint of Palermo.

Rosalind   There is debate about the origins of this name. It may come from the German 'Roslindis', derived from the words for 'horse' and 'snake', or the Spanish 'Rosalinda', meaning 'pretty rose'. Variants include Rosalyn, Rosalynd and Rosalynne. Roslyn is a more recent form.

Rosamund, Rosamond   May be from the German for 'horse protection' or from the Latin for either 'rose of the world' or 'clean rose'. A French form is Rosemonde and a Bulgarian form Rozamunda. The name came to Britain with the Norman Conquest.

Rosanna, Roseanna   Rosanna, a compound of Rose and Anne, has been around for two centuries. Variants include Rosana, Rosannah, Roseana and Roseannah. Rosanne is a more recent version.

Rosanne   A more recent form of Rosanna; also Roseann and Rosan.

Rose, Rosa   After the plant with beautiful flowers and prickly stems, genus *Rosa*, family *Rosaceae*. The name came to Britain in the thirteenth century with the Normans, and had become popular in the nineteenth century in many English-speaking countries, including Australia. Rosa is the Latin form. Variant forms include the Slovakian Ruza, Russian Roza, Ruza and Ruzha, French Rosette and the Spanish Rosita, Rosario, Chara and Charo.

Rosemary   From the herb, whose name came from the Latin *ros* for 'dew', and *marinus* for 'sea'. Variants Rosemarie, Rosemaree.

Rosette   A French form of Rose.

Rosie, Rosy   Diminutive of Rosemary or other 'Rose' names.

Roxanne, Roxanna   From the Persian for 'dawn'. The wife of Alexander the Great was called Roxanne. Also Roxane and Roxana.

Roxie, Roxy   Diminutive of Roxanne or Roxanna.

Roza   Russian and Polish form of Rose.

Ruby   A jewel name, after the red precious stone, and also used to refer to the deep red colour. Ruby Langford Ginibi is an Aboriginal Australian writer.

Rula   A Polish name for girls.

Runako   A Shona name from Africa meaning 'beauty'.

Ruth   A Hebrew name about whose origin scholars are uncertain; it possibly means 'friend' or 'companion'. Ruth Cracknell is a respected Australian actor. The diminutive is Ruthie.

Ruza, Ruzena, Ruzenka   Czechoslovakian forms of Rose.

Ryann, Ryanne   Irish surname of unclear derivation which has been used as a personal name for boys and, more recently, girls.

Ryba   A Czechoslovakian name for girls, meaning 'fish'.

S

Sabina   From the Latin for 'of the Sabines'. The Sabines were a people occupying a part of central Italy. The French forms of the name are Sabine and Sabienne.

Sabrina   The name of an illegitimate daughter of an English king, after whom the Romans named the Severn River.

Sacha   An alternative form of Sasha.

Saffron   After the spice which is taken from the orange stigmas of a purple crocus flower. Saffron the colour is a deep yellow-orange, and is often used to describe religious robes. The short form is Saffi.

Sage   From the Latin word meaning 'wise' or after the aromatic herb.

Sakura   Japanese name for girls, meaning 'cherry blossom'.

Salaidh   Scottish form of Sally.

Salima   Muslim name meaning 'glad, peaceful'.

Sally   This name was originally a diminutive of Sarah but has been used as a completely independent name for some time. The short form is Sal.

Sam   Diminutive of Samantha.

Samantha   Of uncertain origins. May be from the Aramaic, Hebrew for 'listen' or 'listener', or a feminine form of Samuel. Diminutives are Sam, Sammy and Sammie.

Samuela   Feminine form of Samuel.

Sandra   This name was originally the short form of Alessandra. See Alexandra.

Sandy   Short form of Sandra. Sometimes used as an independent name. See Alexandra.

Sapphire   A jewel name from the Greek for 'blue'.

Sara   Alternative form of Sarah now common in Australia. It is used in various European countries.

Sarah   From a Hebrew name meaning 'princess'. Sarah was Abraham's wife; the derivation of her name is found in Genesis. Sally was originally a diminutive but is now firmly established as a name in its own right.

Saranna   A compound of Sarah and Anne, popular in the 1700s.

Sarlote   A Latvian form of Charlotte.

Sasha, Sacha, Sascha Russian short form of Alexander, mainly given to boys.

Satomi Japanese girls, name meaning 'village'.

Savannah, Savanna, Savanah From the Spanish for 'from the treeless plain'.

Scarlett, Scarlet From Middle English for a brilliant deep red. Popularised by the character Scarlett O'Hara in the book and the film *Gone with the Wind*.

Selena, Selina, Seline Of disputed origins. Possibly taken from the Greek word *selene* for 'moon' (one of the alternative names for the moon goddess Artemis), or from the French name Céline.

Seraphina, Serefina Derived from the Hebrew word *seraph*, signifying 'burning intensity'. Serafina is from Spain and Italy; Seraphine is French.

Serena From the Latin for 'serene, calm'.

Shakti A Hindu name for girls.

Shane A form of Jane. Also Shayne, Shayna, Shaini.

Shannon From the Irish Gaelic for 'old' or 'wise', this is the name of an Irish river which became a surname and is now used as a name for boys and girls.

Sharai Hebrew 'princess'. Popular Israeli form of Sarah.

Shareen Arabic name meaning 'sweet as sugar'.

Shari A Hungarian version of Sarah.

Sharon, Sharyn, Sharren From the Hebrew for 'flat plain', or related to Sharai, Sarah. Variants include Sharren, Sharyn, Shari.

Sheena, Shena Popular Irish form of Janet or Jane, which is probably from an anglicisation of Sìne (itself a variant of Sinead).

Sheila, Sheelagh, Shelagh, Sheilah Derived from the Irish name Sile, itself a variant of Celia. Sheila became a slang word in Australia for a female.

Shelby A placename from the Old English for 'the ledge estate'. Also for males. Variant forms are Shelbi and Shellby; the pet form is Shell.

Shelley A placename from the Old English for 'from the meadow on the ledge'. The pet form is Shell.

Sheridan Frances Sheridan was an early British woman novelist, her *Memoirs of Miss Sidney Biddulph* were published in 1761. Her better-known son Richard Brinsley Sheridan produced the comedy *School for Scandal* in 1777, incorporating several events from his mother's novel. The surname Sheridan is now used as a personal name for either sex.

Sherry, Sherri, Sherrie Of disputed origins. After the drink, or a diminutive of an 'Sh' name.

Shirley From the Old English for 'from the bright meadow'. A placename and surname. The diminutive is Shirl.

Shona Feminine form of John.

Shoshana Hebrew form of Susan, 'a lily'. Also Shushanah, Shosha.

Sian The Welsh form of Jane.

Sibyl, Cybil, Sybil, Sybilla According to Greek mythology the sibyls were oracles who uttered prophecies. The German form is Sibylle.

Sidney, Sydney An old English family name now used as a personal name for boys and girls. However the Irish girls' name Sidonie may possibly be the source of its use as a girls' name in Ireland.

Sidonie Irish name possibly originating from the Greek *sindon*, meaning 'linen' or from the Latin for 'woman of Sidon'. Variants are Sidney, Sidonia and Sidony.

Siena, Sienna After the Italian placename. Also a brownish-yellow natural substance (raw sienna), which, when burnt, creates a rich red-brown pigment (burnt sienna).

Sigrid   A popular Scandinavian name from the Old Norse for 'glorious victory'.

Sile, Sisile   Irish forms of Celia, which in turn gave rise to Sheila, Sheelagh.

Silvaine   French form of Sylvia.

Silvana   Italian form of Sylvia.

Silvia   See Sylvia.

Simka   A Hebrew name, meaning 'rejoice'.

Simona   Feminine form of Simon.

Simone   French feminine form of Simon (from the Hebrew for 'listening'). Simone de Beauvoir was a French writer, intellectual, feminist and prominent Existentialist. French variant Simonette, Italian form Simonetta.

Sìne   Variant of the Irish name Sinead. Sheena is probably the anglicised form.

Sinéad   An Irish name which is a diminutive of the French Jehanne or Jeannette, the Irish Gaelic equivalent of Jane. Sinead is quite popular outside of Ireland. Shinae is another spelling. Variant Sìne, related to Sheena.

Siobhan, Shiobain, Shivain, Siban   Another Irish name to come from French name Jehanne or Jeanne, brought to Ireland in the twelfth century by the Anglo-Normans.

Sky, Skye   After the sky, or the island of Skye off Scotland.

Solange   A French name which is derived from the Latin for 'solemn'.

Solveig   A Norse name. Solveig (or Solvejg) is the name of the faithful heroine of Ibsen's lyric drama *Peer Gynt*.

Sonia, Sonya, Sonja   Russian, Slavic and Scandinavian

forms of Sophia imported in the 1920s to Britain.

Sophia From the Greek for 'wisdom'. One of the
several St Sophias had three daughters called Faith,
Hope and Charity. Used in Britain since the 1600s.
Many other forms, including Sophy, Sophie; Slavic
form Zofia; Russian forms Sofya and Sofka.

Sophie Common anglicised form of Sophia. Also the
French form of the name.

Sorcha An Old Irish girls' name meaning 'bright'.

Souline French girls' name; also Soule.

Stacey, Stacy, Stacie Short form of Anastasia, also
used in its own right.

Stamatia Greek form of Samantha.

Stefania Czechoslovakian form of Stephanie,
diminutive Stefka.

Stefanie Form of Stephanie, with diminutive Steffi.

Steffi Diminutive of Stefanie.

Stella Latin for 'star'. A literary name devised by Sir
Philip Sidney to address a woman in a sonnet; it
was later used by Swift.

Stéphane A French form of Stephanie.

Stephanie From the Greek for 'crown' or 'garland'.
Feminine form of Stephen. Short form Stephie.
Many foreign forms, including the Polish Stefaniá
and diminutives Stefciá, Stefká and Stefá. The
Russian form is Stefania, with diminutives Stesha
and Steshda.

Stevie An abbreviation of Steven, sometimes used as
a girls' name.

Sue The most common diminutive of Susan.

Summer After the season.

Sunday After the day of the week. Sunday Reed was
a prominent figure in the Australian art world in the
late 1950s and early 1960s.

Susan, Suzanne From Shushanah (and Shoshanah),

the Hebrew names meaning 'lily'. Older variants
are Susanna, Susannah and Suzanna. Suzanne and
Suzette are forms imported from France.
Diminutives are Susi, Suzi and Susie; the most
common is Sue.

Susanna, Susannah, Suzanna   These were the first
forms of Susan used in Britain in the Middle Ages.

Suzette   French form of Susan.

Svetlana   Russian name for girls. The diminutive is
Svetla.

Sybil, Sybilla   Form of Sibyl.

Sydney   See Sidney.

Sylvia, Silvia   From the Latin for a person who lived in
the wood or forest. Pet form Sylvie, variants Silvana
and Sylvan.

T

Tabitha   From the Greek for 'gazelle'. Short forms
Tab, Tabbi and Tabby.

Tacy, Tacey   Pet form of Tacita, from the Latin for
'silent, quiet'.

Tamar   From the Hebrew, meaning 'date palm tree'.
A biblical name, found in the Old Testament.

Tamara   The Russian form of Tamar, which has
overtaken it in popularity. The name is very popular
with Slavonic families, in Spanish-speaking
countries and in America. Russian forms are Tama,
Tamarka and Tamochka. A Czechoslovakian
diminutive is Mara.

Tammy, Tammi   Diminutives of Tamara and Tamsin.

Tamsin, Tamasin   Feminine diminutives of Thomas

(from the Aramaic for 'twin'). Short form Tammy.

Tania, Tanya   Russian diminutives of Tatiana, which are also names in their own right.

Tanisha   From the Hausa of Africa, meaning 'Monday's child'.

Tansy   From the flower name, which is derived from the Greek *athanasia*, meaning 'everlasting life'.

Tara   Irish Gaelic name, meaning 'rocky hill'. It refers to a hill near Dublin which was reputed to be the home of ancient Irish kings.

Tasha   A Russian name which is a diminutive form of Natasha, used as an independent name.

Tasia   Variant of Tasha.

Tatiana   A Russian name, whose diminutive Tanya has come to be an independent name. St Tatiana was a Christian martyr. Variants include Czechoslovakian forms Tatana and Tana and Polish Taciana, Tola and Tana. Some of the Russian forms include Tatyana, Tanechka, Tanka, Tanya, Tata, Tatka and Tuska.

Taylor, Tayla   An occupational surname, referring to a 'tailor'. Previously used occasionally as a boys' name, but also used as a girls' name.

Tegan, Teagen   A Welsh name meaning 'beautiful'.

Tegwen   Variant of Tegan, meaning 'beautiful' and 'fair'.

Teresa, Theresa   Of uncertain origins, this name may be from the Greek for 'reaper', or derived from the Greek island name 'Therasia'. Famous bearers of the name were two Carmelite nuns, the Spanish St Teresa of Avila, whose popularity spread the name in the sixteenth century, and St Thérèse of Lisieux, who was known as 'The Little Flower', and died in 1897. Variants of the name include the Italian Tersa and Teresina; the Czechoslovakian Terezia, Terezie,

Terezka and Reza; and the German Theresia and Trescha.

Terry, Terri, Teri Short forms of Teresa, also regarded as names in their own right.

Tess A form of Tessa ('fourth child') or Theresa ('reaper'), made popular by Thomas Hardy's heroine in *Tess of the D'Urbervilles*.

Tessa From the Greek, meaning 'fourth child'. Tess is a short form.

Thea From the Greek word for 'divine' and also a diminutive of Dorothea.

Theadora A Greek name meaning 'God's gift'. Bulgarian forms are Teodora and Feodora, Greek form Thedoros, and Polish forms Teodora, Tosia, Dora and Tola.

Thuy Vietnamese name for either sex meaning 'nice, amiable'.

Tiffany From the Greek meaning 'god's appearance', it was given traditionally to children born at the time of the epiphany, when the Magi first saw the Christ Child.

Tikva, Tikvah An Israeli name meaning 'hope'.

Tilda Diminutive of Matilda.

Tilly Short form of Matilda.

Tina A diminutive of Christina or any name ending in 'tina', also used as a name in its own right.

Toby From the Hebrew meaning 'God is good'.

Toni, Tonia Short forms of Antonia.

Tori, Tory Either a diminutive of Victoria or from the Japanese for 'bird'.

Tracey, Tracy Of uncertain etymology. It may be a form of Teresa, or be derived from a surname which meant 'from Thrace'.

Treasa An Irish name for girls which may mean 'strength'.

Trinh   A Vietnamese name for girls.

Triona, Trina   Short forms of Catriona or Caitriona.

Trisha, Tricia   Diminutives of Patricia.

Trixie   A familiar form of Beatrice.

Tyler   From the Middle English, occupational surname for 'a tiler'.

U

Udele   Old English feminine of the Teutonic boys' name Otto, meaning prosperous, affluent.

Ulrica   From the Old German, meaning 'ruler'.

Uma   A Hindi Sanskrit name for 'light' and 'peace'.

Una, Oona, Oonagh   An Old Irish name of uncertain origin. A variant is Juno.

Undine, Undina, Ondine   From the Latin for 'of the waves'. Undine is a water sprite in Roman mythology.

Unity   Unity (as in 'oneness') is another of the abstract quality or 'virtue' names favoured by the Puritans after the Reformation.

Urania   From the Greek for 'heavenly'. In Greek mythology Urania was the muse who presided over astronomy.

Urbana   From the Latin *urbanus*, meaning 'of the town'.

Ursula   From the Latin for 'little she-bear'. St Ursula was a favourite saint in the Middle Ages. She was said to have been slain with 11,000 virgins by Atilla the Hun, with an order of nuns being named after her. The name is used in many countries in many forms. Ursella is a variant. The Romanian form is

Ursule; Latvian form Urzula; Polish form Urszula;
and French form Ursule.

Urzula   Latvian form of Ursula.

Uta   A German name of uncertain derivation.

Utopia   A literary invention by Sir Thomas Moore
for the title and subject of his major political essay
about an ideal form of government and society.
The word comes from the Greek for 'good' or 'no
place'.

Uyen   Vietnamese name for girls meaning 'elegant,
harmonious'.

V

Val   Diminutive of Valerie, Valentine, Valentina.

Valentine, Valentina   From the Latin for 'robust and
strong'. A third-century Roman priest, Valentinus,
was beheaded and became a Christian martyr.
The pagan festival was transferred to the saint's
day and St Valentine's Day was created. Valentina
is a form used only for girls. Pet forms are Val
and Valli.

Valerie, Vallerie, Valery   After the name of an old
Roman family, derived from the Latin *valere*, 'to be
strong'. The French form Valérie was imported from
France to England as Valerie at the end of the last
century. The Italian form is Valeria. Diminutives
Valli and Val.

Valeska   A Slavic name meaning 'illustrious leader'.

Valma, Valmai   A Welsh name for girls meaning
'mayflower'.

Valya, Valka   Russian names for girls.

Vanda Variant of Wanda, from the Old German.

Vanessa Of disputed origins; said to be a literary invention of eighteenth-century writer Jonathan Swift for a woman called Esther Vanhomrigh, but also associated with the Greek Phanessa, meaning 'butterfly'.

Vanetta Probably a variant of Vanessa.

Vanna A Cambodian name for both boys and girls.

Vanni Italian form of Anne, or pet form of Vanessa.

Varinka A Russian form of Vera.

Varvara A Russian form of Barbara.

Vashti Probably from the Persian for 'beautiful'. Found in the Bible.

Veda A variant of Vida. The name also refers to the four sacred books of Hindu knowledge.

Venus After the Roman goddesss of love.

Vera From the Russian for 'faith', sometimes held to be from the Latin word for 'truth'. Found particularly in Slavic countries. Russian forms Verasha, Verinka and Verka.

Verity From the Latin word that means 'truth'. Another Puritan abstract quality or 'virtue' name.

Veronica From the Latin for 'a true image'. The original 'true image' was said to be that of Jesus Christ, on a cloth used by a woman to wipe his face as he carried his cross to Calvary. The name came to be associated with the woman. The French form is Véronique; the German Veronike; the Hungarian Veronika. The name is associated with Berenice. Short forms include Ron, Ronny, Ronnie, Vonny, Vonnie and Nicky.

Vesta The Roman goddess of the hearth, who was worshipped in each Roman household, and also in a circular Temple in the Forum, with a sacred fire tended by the six Vestal Virgins.

Vicki, Vicky, Vikki   Pet forms of Victoria.

Victoria, Viktoria   From the Latin, meaning 'victory'. The name was commonly used by the first Christians in the Roman Empire, and has had various surges of popularity since then. Queen Victoria (1837–1901) was the first famous British woman of this name, and the Australian state was named after her. Pet forms include Vicky, Vickie and Vikki.

Victorine   A French variation of Victoria, this is in fact the feminine of Victor ('conqueror').

Vida   Originally a diminutive of Davida, now often used in its own right. Also Veda.

Villette   A French name meaning 'a small town'.

Viola   Latin name meaning 'violet', after the flower. Short form Vi.

Violet   A flower name, derived from the Latin *viola*. The short form is Vi; the French form is Violetta. Related to Viola, Yolette, Yolande, Yolanda and Yolanthe.

Violetta   The French form of Violet.

Virginia   Originally derived from a Roman clan name, Verginius, it was later assumed to come from the Latin *virgo* for 'maiden, virgin'. The name of a state in America, in honour of Queen Elizabeth I. Virginia Woolf was the famous innovative British novelist at the centre of the Bloomsbury circle. Pet forms of the name include Ginny, Jinny. The French form is Virginie.

Vita   Pet form of Davita or Victoria, or from the Italian for 'life'.

Vittoria   Italian variant of Victoria.

Viveca, Vivecka   From the Latin, an alternative form of Vivien.

Vivian, Vivien, Vyvyan, Vyvian   From the Latin name

Vivianus, itself possibly from *vivus*, meaning 'alive,
living'. Viviana is a variant from the Middle Ages.
French form Vivienne.

Viviana Variant of Vivian.

Vivienne French form of Vivian.

Volska Greek form of Barbara.

Vondra A Czechoslovakian name meaning 'a loving
woman'.

Voula A Greek name for girls.

Wallis A variant of Wallace, a personal name which
came from a surname associated with the Saxon
word *waelisc* for 'stranger' or 'foreigner', which was
applied to Celts in England. Short forms include
Wally and Wal.

Wanda Probably from the Old German for
'wanderer'. Some sources associate it with Wendy.

Wendy, Wendie J.M. Barrie created this name, said
to be taken from a name given to him by a little
girl, *fwendy* (an attempt at 'friendy'), which led to
Wendy. Wendy Darling was a character in his
1904 play *Peter Pan*. Some sources suggest the
name is a familiar form of Gwendolyn and
Wanda.

Wenona From the Old German for 'provider of joy'.
(Not associated with Winona.)

Whitney From the Anglo-Saxon for 'white island'.

Wilhelmina Feminine form of the German Wilhelm
(William), a compound of 'will' and 'helmet'.
Imported to Britain in the nineteenth century.

Wilma and Willa are variants, Mina, Minna and Minny are diminutives.

Willa   Variant form of Wilhelmina.

Willow   Middle English after 'the willow tree'.

Wilma   A variant of Wilhemina.

Winifred   Derived from the Old English for 'friend of peace', which was an anglicisation of the name of a Welsh saint. In the first century AD St Winifred was proposed to by Prince Caractacus, said 'No', and had her head cut off. Winnie and Win are pet forms of the name.

Winnie   Diminutive of Winifred.

Winona   A Native American name meaning 'first-born daughter'. (Not associated with Wenona.)

Wyn, Wynne   From the Welsh for 'fair' or 'white'.

X

Xandra   Spanish form of Zandra. See Alexandra.

Xanthe   A Greek name meaning 'blonde', yellow-haired'. Xanthia is a variant.

Xaviera, Xaverie   Feminine forms of Xavier, a Basque name meaning 'new home owner'.

Xena   A Greek name meaning 'hospitable'. Also Xenia, Zena, Zenia.

Xuan   A Vietnamese name for girls.

Xylia   A Greek form of Sylvia. Also Xylina.

Y

Yaffah   A Hebrew name meaning 'attractive woman'.

Yang   Chinese 'sun'.

Yarina, Yaryna   Russian forms of Irene.

Yashoda   A Hindu name meaning 'one who gives success', the mother of Krishna.

Yasmin, Yasmina   Arabic forms of Jasmine. Other Arabic variants are Yasmeen and Yasiman.

Yasuko   A Japanese name for girls meaning 'safe'.

Yehudit   Biblical Jewish name, a form of Judith.

Yessica   Hebrew alternative form of Jessica.

Yetta   Short form of Henrietta. Also Yette.

Yohanah   A Hebrew form of Joanna. Also Yoanna, Yohanka.

Yolanda, Yolande   Greek name meaning 'the violet flower'. Also Yolana, Yolane. Related to Olanthe, Olinda. French form Yolande, variant Yolette.

Yonina, Yonine, Jonina   A Hebrew name that means 'dove'. Feminine form of Jonah.

Yseulte   A Welsh variant of Isolde.

Yukie   A Japanese name for girls meaning 'happiness'.

Yuko   A Japanese name for girls meaning 'excellent'.

Yuriko   A Japanese name for girls meaning 'lily'.

Yvette   French diminutive of Yvonne, popular as a name in its own right. Also Evette, Ivette.

Yvonne   The feminine form of Ives or Ivo (from the Old German meaning 'yew', which may have signified an archer). Alternative spelling Evonne.

Z

Zada Arabic name meaning 'prosperous lucky'. Also
  Zaidee.
Zainab, Zianabu An Arabic name meaning 'the
  prophet's daughter'.
Zandra See Alexandra.
Zanna Latvian form of Jane.
Zara From the Hebrew, meaning 'dawn'. Also a form
  of Sarah.
Zarita Spanish form of Sarah.
Zdenka A Czechoslovakian name for girls.
Zea Alternative spelling of Zia.
Zelda German, a pet form of Griselda ('grey warrior
  maiden'), often used independently.
Zelena Czechoslovakian name with diminutive
  Zelenka.
Zena A Greek name, a variant of Xenia, and an
  Ethiopian name meaning 'news'.
Zeynep A favourite Turkish name.
Zia From the Latin for 'grain'. Also Zea.
Zilla, Zilah, Zillah Hebrew name meaning 'shade' or
  'shadow', it was the name of one of the wives of
  Lamech in the Old Testament.
Zina A Swahili name meaning 'attractive'.
Zissa A Yiddish name meaning 'sweetie'.
Zoe From the Greek, meaning 'life'.
Zofia, Zofie Forms of Sophie.
Zuhra, Zohra An Islamic name after the star Venus.
Zuleika Arabic name meaning 'brilliant one'.
Zuriel Hebrew name meaning 'god is my rock'.
Zuzana Czechoslovakian and Polish form of Susan
  with diminutives Zuzankà, Zuzkà and Zusà.
Zytka A nice Polish name for 'a rose'.